How to Make
SUSHI
at Home

How to Make SUSHI at Home

A Fundamental Guide for Beginners and Beyond

Jun and Stephanie Nakajima

Skyhorse Publishing

Copyright © 2023 by Jun and Stephanie Nakajima

Skyhorse Publishing books may be purchased in bulk at special discounts for sales promotion, corporate gifts, fund-raising, or educational purposes. Special editions can also be created to specifications. For details, contact the Special Sales Department, Skyhorse Publishing, 307 West 36th Street, 11th Floor, New York, NY 10018 or info@skyhorsepublishing.com.

Skyhorse® and Skyhorse Publishing® are registered trademarks of Skyhorse Publishing, Inc.®, a Delaware corporation.

Visit our website at www.skyhorsepublishing.com.

10 9 8 7 6 5 4 3 2 1

Library of Congress Cataloging-in-Publication Data is available on file.

Cover design by David Ter-Avanesyan
Cover photo credit: Jun and Stephanie Nakajima

Print ISBN: 978-1-5107-7350-9
Ebook ISBN: 978-1-5107-7351-6

Printed in China

Contents

Introduction

Sushi is by far the most well-known Japanese cuisine and has become extremely popular at a global scale. What used to be available only in Japanese restaurants is now readily available in a variety of food establishments—grocery stores, school cafeterias, even gas stations. Depending on where you live, the sushi you're familiar with could be quite different than the authentic and traditional style originated in Japan. But that's the beauty of it. The concept of sushi has grown so multicultrally that there's new and interesting "fusion" creations all the time. Although I respect and love the tradition of Japanese sushi, it really excites me to see people having fun and exploring new boundaries when making sushi.

Traditionally in Japan, to become a professional sushi chef would require years and years of dedication. The first years were spent meticulously learning and repetitive training on cooking rice and preparing vegetables. Not to mention the cleaning and maintenance of all supplies, equipment, and the restaurant itself. Often you wouldn't even be able to touch the fish until a few years in. Though this tradition has faded away a bit in modern years, the culture still does exist and lives on. And thankfully so, because there's nothing quite like a perfectly crafted piece of nigiri by a traditionally taught master sushi chef. But don't worry, I'm not asking you to dedicate years of your life to learning and crafting your sushi skills.

Sushi is often seen as a very intimidating cuisine that scares even the best chefs. And yes, it is a very complex skill filled with traditional techniques that take years upon years to master. But don't let that discourage you from even trying! I will guide you step-by-step through the fundamentals of sushi and teach you how to take that skill and make it your own.

My twenty-plus years of training as a sushi chef originally started from my dad, who's owned and operated a Japanese restaurant for more than thirty-five years. He taught me all the fundamentals and guided me throughout the first part of my sushi career. I then started my own sushi catering company, which I operated for more than ten years. During this time, I have had the pleasure of working with so many amazing clients. I've also had countless opportunities to teach how to make sushi and I noticed there was a gap—between people who wanted to make sushi but didn't know how to even start, scared to even. That is the reason why I decided to write this book, to share my knowledge and teach the proper fundamentals to those who are curious about making sushi. Because as intimidating as it may be, making sushi is actually quite easy to do at home.

To those who didn't know where to start, well, you chose the right book, and I'm excited for you! This is the start line. I have compiled years of my experience and simplified it into this one single book so that it can be a gateway to your sushi journey. Whether your goal is to make your favorite sushi at home, impress your family and friends with your own sushi creations, or practice to become a professional sushi chef, this book will help you accomplish those goals.

You'll find many of my personal recipes in this book; however, this is not just a recipe book. More so, it is a skills development book, that skill being the art of sushi. Sushi is a unique and amazing cuisine where once you have the basics down, you can let your imagination take over. Take a sushi roll, for example; I can share hundreds of recipes on all different types of rolls and make this book four-hundred-plus pages, but the fundamental techniques for each are very similar. Sure, there's slight differences (which I do teach), but most of it just takes repetition and practice. My goal is to teach you the fundamentals of making sushi, which will allow you to confidently take that skill and dive into the art of sushi on your own. The beauty of sushi, especially making it at home, is in the endless possibilities and the fact that you can do whatever you want.

"If you give a man a fish, you feed him for a day. If you teach a man to fish, you feed him for a lifetime."

Yes, pun intended.

—Jun Nakajima, Summer 2022

P. S. Visit us at www.TheSushiMan.com to learn more about our story.

History

Sushi has evolved throughout centuries before it became that which we know today. Although Japan is the sushi capital of the world, the original concept was said to be founded in southern China, where fish was pickled and fermented by wrapping it with rice, dating all the way back to around the second century. This method was to preserve the fish and the rice was actually thrown out.

It wasn't until about the eighth century that this concept spread to Japan and became known as "narezushi" (matured sushi). When lifestyles evolved, so did the sushi. Narezushi became something called "namanarezushi" where the fish was consumed much earlier (while it was still partially raw) and the rice was also consumed. Fast-forward to the Edo period, between 1603 and 1867 (Edo is what

Example sushi stall from the Edo period from the Edo history museum. (© dreamstime.com / Viocara)

we know as Tokyo today), vinegar started to be used to speed up the fermentation process. The addition of vinegar not only made it immediately consumable but introduced a whole new flavor profile to what sushi was then.

Then around 1820, a man by the name Hanaya Yohei (often referred to as the "founder of sushi") created what's known now as "nigirizushi." Until this point, sushi was either still wrapped in rice or pressed in a box form called "oshizushi." Yohei took the vinegared rice and shaped it into a ball and added the fish on top, which revolutionized the sushi industry. During this time there was no refrigeration yet, so the fish had to be prepared first, often cured with salt, vinegar, or cooked. This became the origin of what we call "Edomaezushi" (Edo-style sushi).

As the years went on, this "new" nigiri-style sushi spread across the country like wildfire and became the standard for all sushi restaurants. At one point it was said that there was an average of one to two sushi restaurants (or stalls) within every couple blocks in Edo. And as refrigeration technology advanced, restaurants opened all throughout the country and eventually expanded worldwide.

FUN FACT—The original nigirizushi was much larger than the typical piece that we see today (almost twice the size). Diners would request it to be cut in half, making it easier to eat. This request was so common that it eventually became the norm. Therefore, nigirizushi is often served in pairs per order.

Sushi was said to be introduced in the United States in the early 1900s and took off in popularity in the 1960s. There's a bit of a debate on which restaurant was truly the first, but one of the most famous was a restaurant by the name of Kawafuku, which was in Little Tokyo of Los Angeles, California.

The concept of eating raw fish was so foreign it took a while for Americans to develop a taste for it. Restaurants had to be creative not only with the type of ingredients they used, but also in the way they made sushi to satisfy the American patron's palates. This is when the "uramaki" was born, where the rice is on the outside of the nori (seaweed) rather than the traditional style with the nori on the outside. This helped minimize the flavor and texture of the nori and became much more popular among American diners. The prime and most well-known example of this is the "California Roll."

Fast-forward to the present, and the plethora of sushi options can be a bit overwhelming at times. But that's how much sushi has evolved. And there's nothing wrong with that, it's the beauty of change and adaptation. What started with a piece of fish inside a rice ball is now a globally consumed culinary art form that showcases the talent and skills of each sushi chef. For those who seek tradition, it still lives on in countless sushi restaurants all around the world. From traditional to modern, there really is something for everyone.

Supplies and Tools

KNIVES

Throughout my many years in the sushi industry, one of the most common questions I get asked is, "what type of knife do you use?" or specifically, "what type of knives are best for making sushi?" A valid question, as I cannot express enough the importance of a good, well-made, sharp knife especially for making sushi.

When searching online, the list of different sushi knives claiming to be the sharpest in the world can be overwhelming. The price can range from $20 to $2,000, sometimes more, which makes it much more confusing and discouraging. No one wants to spend an arm and a leg on a product that will be forgotten in a drawer. So, how do you choose the right knife?

There are a variety of knives used for sushi, and each one serves a different purpose. I want to provide color around the most popular types along with the best use for each style knife. This can be an important purchase as you start your sushi journey, so ask yourself a few questions:

- How serious am I about making sushi? (Is this for fun or are you trying make it a profession?)
- How often will I be making sushi?
- Do I want to use this knife for other types of cuisines?
- How much do I want to spend?

Although there are many factors to consider when defining a good knife—sharpness, size, shape, weight, feel, what type of steel, edge retention, ease of maintenance, etc.—and though there are basic components that all good knives should have, it really comes down to personal preference and how you're going to be using it day to day. I'll go over the most popular styles of knives (used for sushi) and explain how each one may best fit your needs.

Yanagiba (The Traditional Sushi Knife)

In Japanese, "yanagiba" translates to "willow leaf blade" and refers to the long and narrow leaves from a willow tree. These knives are the standard and most used in the sushi industry. The long blade allows for a smooth, clean cut when slicing boneless fish and is also great for cutting vegetables. And like many traditional Japanese knives, it is a single-bevel blade (sharpened on one side only), which can achieve a finer and sharper edge but can take some practice to get used to. The single bevel also means that it is *not* universal for right- and left-handed users.

> **NOTE**—If you decide to purchase this type of knife, be sure to get the correct sided bevel.

The best uses for a yanagiba are cutting sashimi, fish for nigiri, de-skinning fish, and cutting makizushi or rolls. However, it's not the best for all-around cooking, the blade is too long for general cutting jobs and since most traditional yanagibas are made of carbon steel it can be brittle, which means stay away from anything hard or that has thick bones.

> **PRO TIP**—Carbon steel knives are usually preferred among professionals mainly because of how extremely sharp the edge can get and retain it for a longer period. However, it is not the easiest to maintain and is vulnerable to rust and stains if not taken care of properly.

Sujihiki (The Sushi Knife of the West)

The "sujihiki" is the Western-style version of the yanagiba. Instead of a single-bevel blade like the yanagiba, it is double-beveled, which means it's sharpened down from both sides of the blade (a characteristic of Western knives). The size and shape are very similar to the yanagiba as well as the uses. It is perfect for slicing sashimi or any boneless fish, as well as carving boneless meats. The single-bevel yanagiba still has the upper hand when it comes to sharpness, but the sujihiki might be more comfortable and easier to use for those used to Western knives. It is still extremely sharp and retains its edge well. Sujihikis can come in all different types of steel including high carbon and stainless.

> **NOTE**—A stainless-steel blade won't require as much care versus carbon steel, but it won't be as sharp either.

Gyuto (The All-Around Chef Knife)

If you're looking for one all-around knife that does it all, this is it. The gyuto, which directly translates to "cow blade," is the Japanese version of the classic Western-style chef's knife. It was originally used to cut and break down beef and is one of the most versatile knives out there. It's great for slicing, chopping, mincing, or dicing anything from fish, to meats, veggies, or fruits. But since the blade is thinner and lighter compared to a Western chef's knife, you want to stay away from bones or anything hard.

The gyuto could be a great option if you're looking for a knife that can be used for all types of cuisines. We use our gyuto for about 90 percent of our home cooking, while my yanagiba and sujihiki is primarily for professional work. I often use the gyuto to cut fish for sushi as well. It comes in a variety of different steels just like the sujihiki.

Deba (The Muscle Knife)

The deba is a thick and sturdy knife used for breaking down a whole fish. Its heavy and durable blade can behead the fish and cut through the bones, as well as fillet it with precision thanks to its fine tip. You can also use it to break down poultry or other meats with small bones. But it is not a cleaver, so stay away from any meats that have larger bones.

Traditional deba knives are single beveled and hold a razor-sharp edge. But that means it can feel a bit awkward if you're not used to it, just like the yanagiba. It's a great knife and crucial to have if you're in the sushi industry, but I wouldn't recommend it for every day, at-home use (unless you're planning on breaking down

From top (clockwise)—Yanagiba, Gyuto, Deba, Sujihiki

whole fish all the time). If you are or planning on becoming a professional sushi chef, then I highly recommend having one, but only after you have a quality yanagiba or sujihiki (either one of those would come first).

Summary

Again, the most important thing is to figure out how you're going to be using the knife. If you're serious about making sushi, consider a yanagiba or sujihiki and then possibly a deba afterward. If you want a versatile knife that you can use for other types of cooking, go for the gyuto.

As for the material and type of steel, stay away from high carbon if you know you're not going to meticulously maintain it. Something that is stainless (or a hybrid of stainless and carbon) will be much easier to take care of and probably better for general home use. On the other hand, if you know how to take care of knives (or learn how to) and don't mind the extra care, go for carbon steel. It is more expensive but worth the investment.

Please note that it's not a requirement to have any of these knives. If you want to use what you have, go for it. But if you find yourself struggling to cut anything and your sushi looks like it's been mauled by a bear, then it might be worth the investment. Remember, a good-quality knife will last you a lifetime if you take care of it.

CUTTING BOARD

The cutting board may seem simple, and, yes, you can use whatever you already have in your kitchen. But what's the point of this book if I don't share my knowledge and opinions, right?

With that said, the best type of cutting board for sushi is the Hi-Soft synthetic board. It's made from a soft polyvinyl acetate material, and it helps minimize the stress on your knife and your hands, all the while being bacteria resistant. You really do notice the difference! It's used mainly in professional settings and is the most popular board among sushi chefs. But it can be a bit pricey and not everyone's willing to invest in one. In my opinion, if you are serious enough to invest in a professional sushi knife, then it's worth looking into. Your knives will thank you!

A Hinoki (Japanese cypress) board is also a great option, plus it smells amazing! It protects the knife edge well due to the medium-soft firmness of the wood along with being durable and highly resistant to bacteria. It does require a bit more maintenance compared to the Hi-Soft board, but you really can't go wrong with either.

Other types of boards can work as well. Wooden boards are recommended over plastic (or glass), but use whatever you have and test it out for yourself. Just like the knives, if you're serious about making sushi or know that you'll be using it enough, then it might be worth the investment. Also, you can use these cutting boards for your daily cooking. It doesn't have to be designated for sushi-making only.

PRO TIP—A cutting board (especially a lighter one) can often move when you're working on it. This can be very dangerous and affect your cuts. To avoid this, you can simply put a lightly damp towel under the board (be sure the surface underneath is waterproof) to create a friction pad. Rubber grip liners work as well.

RICE COOKER

There are a couple of ways to cook rice. If you have an electric rice cooker, this will be the most convenient option, though such a device is not required. If you don't own one, turn to page 82 for the stovetop method. I go over step-by-step on how to make the perfect sushi rice using a pot on the stove.

SUSHI OKE / HANGIRI (WOODEN SUSHI MIXING BOWL)

Another tool that is not required but will up your sushi game is the sushi oke, also called hangiri. It's a wooden (usually cypress or cedar) tub that's used to mix sushi vinegar with cooked rice. It allows the rice to cool properly while absorbing some of the vinegar, which results in better texture and consistency. If you do decide to get one, be sure to read the Sushi Oke Maintenance section at the end of this chapter (see page 11). It's not hard, but it can be ruined without proper care. Alternatively, you can simply use a large bowl to mix the vinegar into the rice.

SHAMOJI (RICE PADDLE)

Shamoji is a rice paddle used to mix and scoop the rice. It's mainly used to prepare the sushi rice prior to making sushi. If possible, find one that has an anti-stick surface (which helps keep the rice from sticking) and is dishwasher-safe. It makes the whole process much more convenient, especially if you cook rice a lot. Though not ideal, you can substitute with a wooden spoon or a plastic spatula. I would stay away from soft rubber spatulas.

MAKISU (BAMBOO ROLLING MAT)

If you've ever watched a sushi chef make makizushi or sushi rolls, you've most likely seen a makisu. It's a woven bamboo mat that helps roll, support, and shape the rolls. If you're planning on making any type of roll, then this is a must-have. There are newer types of makisu made from plastic or silicone. In my experience, the traditional bamboo provides the best result, plus bamboo has natural antibacterial qualities. When comparing which one to purchase, look for the style where each bamboo rod is thicker. The skinnier ones tend to be too flexible and makes it more difficult to roll.

> **PRO TIP**—Which side of the makisu to use? Take the makisu (bamboo rolling mat) and look at the individual sticks from the side; some makisu's will have a flat side while the other side is rounded. We want to use the flat side so that our roll ends up with a cleaner shape. Typically, the flat side will be greenish in color while the rounded side is a lighter tan.

OTOSHIBUTA (DROP LID)

An otoshibuta is a drop lid used a lot in Japanese cooking for simmered foods. It helps the ingredients absorb all the flavors evenly while simmering, all the while preventing ingredients from breaking apart.

If you don't own one, you can make an otoshibuta using aluminum foil. Tear a sheet of foil that's about the same diameter as the saucepan. Fold in the edges to make a circular disc that fits just inside the pan. Poke a few holes toward the center (the larger the pan, the more holes you need) and place it inside the pan.

MORIBASHI (PLATING CHOPSTICKS)

Moribashi are long chopsticks that have a stainless-steel tip. They can be used for plating, serving, and garnishing dishes like sushi, sashimi, tempura, decorating foods, etc. It is probably most comparable to tongs but handles smaller food items. Many professional chefs like using these, as the metal tips doesn't hold in the smells of food. These are optional, as you can use regular wooden chopsticks as a substitute.

FISH BONE TWEEZERS

Needless to say what these are, as the name says it all. Yes, there are tweezers made specifically to remove fish bones. They are made with a stronger and better grip versus cosmetic tweezers. Even grocery-bought fish that has been cleaned and cut may have an occasional pin-bone. If you eat fish and purchase your seafood fresh regularly, owning a pair comes in handy.

TAMAGOYAKI FRYING PAN

Tamagoyaki is a traditional Japanese egg omelet that is cooked into a rectangular shape for sushi (see page 214). The square shape of the skillet allows the egg to be cooked with clean edges and corners. It is not very suitable for other cooking though and is not required to make tamagoyaki.

Top (left to right)—sushi oke (hangiri), shamoji (rice paddle), cutting board. Bottom (left to right)—sujihiki, deba, moribashi (plating chopsticks), fish bone tweezers, makisu (bamboo rolling mat)]

SUSHI OKE (HANGIRI) MAINTENANCE

A sushi oke, or what some might call hangiri, is a great thing to have if you plan on making sushi often. Plus, it makes you look that much more professional! But it does require some maintenance, especially in the beginning. Here are the steps to properly season and maintain your sushi oke.

Before first use:

1. Before the first use, you want to properly season the oke. To do this, first rinse out the oke with clean water.
2. Next, fill it up about halfway and add ¼ cup of rice vinegar. Stir and let sit a minimum 2 hours and up to overnight. Try to leave it over a sink or place some kitchen towels under it just in case there's leakage.
3. After soaking, wash it with clean water (no detergents or chemicals).
4. Dry well with a clean towel. Flip it upside down and prop one side up so that it can air dry. Do not leave where sunlight can hit it.

Before each use:

1. Rinse the oke.
2. Fill it about halfway with clean water and let it soak for 20 to 30 minutes.
3. Drain the water and wipe down with a clean, damp towel. There shouldn't be any standing water. It's important to do this for a few reasons. When left too dry, the rice will stick to it like glue and also the wood absorbs too much of the sushi vinegar. If too wet, the extra moisture will mix in with the rice and make it mushy.

After each use:

1. Use a damp cloth to remove the extra rice.
2. Let it soak in warm water to get the remaining rice off. You can use a sponge to remove some of the stubborn grains of rice if needed. Do not use any detergents, chemicals, or any type of steel or wire brush.
3. After washing, make sure to dry the entire oke very thoroughly using a clean towel. Flip it upside-down and prop one side up so that there's air flow underneath. Do not leave where sunlight can hit it. Let dry overnight.

Basic Pantry Ingredients

In addition to the basic everyday pantry ingredients (salt, sugar, flour, etc.), a sushi pantry will need some traditional Japanese ingredients that you might or might not be too familiar with. Below I list some of the standard and important ingredients you'll need to follow the recipes in this book.

RICE

Rice is the most important ingredient when it comes to sushi, because without it, it's not sushi! More on that later when we make the sushi rice (see page 81). But to make good sushi, you must have good (correct) rice. Now I understand picking the right rice can be a bit overwhelming, especially when you consider there are more than 120,000 varieties of rice in the world and on top of that numerous brands out there. But I'll keep it very simple, just stick to Japanese short- or medium-grain rice and you should be fine. It doesn't necessarily have to be grown in Japan. There are several high-quality Japanese rice brands that are grown in California both short and medium grain. Both have a natural stickiness that makes it perfect for sushi, but short grain does result in a better texture and consistency. Avoid using any long-grain rice such as basmati or jasmine. These types of rice will be too dry and won't be sticky enough for sushi.

RICE VINEGAR

Rice vinegar is used to make sushi vinegar. It's also used to make what's called "tezu" or "temizu" which is a mixture of water and rice vinegar used to dampen our hands while we make sushi. It's not a necessity but it helps keep the flavor of the sushi more consistent.

> **PRO TIP**—Tezu—sometimes called temizu—is a mixture of water and rice vinegar we use to wet our hands throughout the sushi-making (especially nigiri) process. Vinegar helps keep the flavor of the sushi rice consistent and it also helps kill off any bacteria that may be on our hands. When making mixture, pour roughly 2 ounces of vinegar per 6–8 ounces of water.

If you would like to keep things simple, you can purchase seasoned rice/sushi vinegar that is ready to use. However, making your own sushi vinegar is easy! I teach you how to make this with my own recipe on page 86. If you decide to make your own, make sure you purchase unseasoned rice vinegar. Some well-known brands in the United States are Marukan, Kikkoman, and Mizkan. All are good options.

NORI (DRIED SEAWEED)

Nori is an item that can be much more complicated to pick out than it should be. There is an abundance of different options and there is no standard industry grading, making it hard to figure out which one is best for sushi. Generally, most options are of good quality, so it really comes down to personal preference and a little trial and error.

The different grades for sushi nori can be confusing since different brands have their own grading levels. You should typically see either a color or alphabet grading system. The alphabet grading is straightforward, "A" being the best, "B" second, and so forth till usually "D." The color system is a bit more complex, as different brands have their own system, but typically it's ranked in this order: Gold, Silver (or blue), Green (or yellow), and then Red. Pay attention to the packaging color, which usually will correspond with the grade level. You can also compare it by price, as long as it's the same brand.

Some simple ways to tell if sushi nori is of good quality are by the actual color of the nori, thickness, and sheen. The higher the grade, the darker the color (closer to black), while lower grades will be green or light green. This goes hand in hand with the thickness as well. Lower grades will be light and almost translucent while higher grades will be dense and solid. Higher quality nori will also have a sheen to it, making it look shiny.

Most sushi nori comes in either full or half sheets. Full sheets are right around 8" × 7" and the half sheets are the same but just precut in half. Half sheets are what's used for the majority of sushi rolls so I usually recommend those, but you can always cut them yourself if you can only find the full sheets.

SHOYU (SOY SAUCE)

Shoyu or soy sauce to sushi, is like butter to bread. It just goes together. Feel free to use your favorite brand. Keep in mind, using too much soy sauce tends to overpower the sushi flavor itself.

Personally, I recommend making what's called "nikiri" or "nikiri shoyu." You might have seen sushi chefs brush it on top of a freshly made nigiri if you've sat at the sushi bar (typically at higher-end restaurants). I share my simple recipe on page 19. But basically, it's a mixture of soy sauce, mirin (sweet rice wine), dashi, and sake (rice wine). The flavor is sweeter and has more depth than soy sauce on its own. It also has a thicker consistency. A little can go a long way; brushing a little on top of the sushi is perfect.

Left to right: Top row—wasabi, katsuobushi, konbu. Middle row—gari, short grain rice. Bottom row—goma, nori, unseasoned rice vinegar, and soy sauce

WASABI

Most people know wasabi as the spicy green paste that automatically comes with sushi, and eating too much of it will clear your sinuses better than most cold medicines. But what is wasabi exactly? Wasabi is a root (rhizome, to be exact) that is notoriously difficult to grow. It needs to be in the perfect climate and takes years to grow to full size, which makes it very limited and very expensive. For that reason, most of the wasabi that we see at restaurants (even in Japan) is not real "hon" wasabi. So, what are we all eating? It's a mixture of horse-radish, mustard, and green food coloring.

If you're an avid sushi lover and have an opportunity to try real "hon" wasabi, I highly recommend you try it at least once. But fair warning, you might not want to go back to the imitation stuff ever again!

Real wasabi is a lot milder than its imitation version. The texture is a bit gritty (little, tiny chunks left from grating) and it has a subtle sweetness with fresh green and herb aromas. There's really nothing like it, especially when it's freshly grated and served with the perfect bite of sashimi or nigiri.

That said, there's nothing wrong with imitation wasabi, and the store-bought ones work just fine. The ones in the tube are more convenient. Wasabi powder is also available and has a longer shelf life versus the tube.

If you want to get adventurous, kizami wasabi (chopped wasabi) is another form of wasabi that goes very well with sushi and is one of my personal favorites. It's made from the stems of real "hon" wasabi, which is chopped up and marinated in soy sauce. It has a slight crunchy texture and perfect amount of spiciness. It typically comes in small packs either refrigerated or frozen. Kinjirushi is a good brand.

GARI (PICKLED GINGER)

Alongside the wasabi is usually a small mound of pickled ginger or "gari." It is used to cleanse the palate between different types of sushi so that you can enjoy each piece to its fullest flavor. The slight sweetness and spiciness of gari "cuts" the richness of the fish and eliminates any leftover taste. Think of it as a reset for your tongue. Ginger also has bacteria-fighting components and is said to help with stomach pains.

Pickled ginger should be easy to find at your local grocery store or Asian markets. If you plan on making sushi vinegar, you can use this to pickle your own ginger. I show you how on page 220.

GOMA (SESAME SEEDS)

Toasted sesame seeds add extra flavor, texture, and are used a lot in sushi rolls. If you enjoy sesame seeds and want to take it up a level, I recommend using a sesame seed grinder. Grinding the seeds will bring out much more

of the aroma while crushing the seeds to your preferred size. I have had past catering customers rave about ground sesame seeds and how they can't go back. Try it for yourself and see what you think. You can find analog and battery-powered sesame street grinders.

DASHI (JAPANESE STOCK)

Dashi is a soup stock that is the basis of many Japanese dishes; think of it as the mother of umami. Unlike a lot of Western soup stock where it's typical to simmer meats for long hours, Japanese dashi is extremely simple and usually consists of only one or two ingredients. Here are some of the most common ingredients dashi is made of:

- **Konbu (dried kelp)**—Vegan- and vegetarian-friendly, this type of dashi is one of the most common and easy to make. Look for it in the dried seaweed section at your local Asian grocery store.
- **Katsuobushi (dried bonito flakes)**—This is one of my personal favorites. It's so versatile and gives an elegant, umami-packed flavor that goes well with so many dishes. It's really simple to use as well. You literally just toss it in some water and strain it. It can also be used for toppings on hiyayakko (cold tofu), ohitashi (Japanese spinach salad), and so much more. You should be able to find it in a similar section as the konbu.
- **Dried shiitake mushroom**—Also vegan- and vegetarian-friendly. Gives out a good umami flavor by itself but is better combined with katsuo or konbu dashi.

You can also find dashi powder that you simply add into any soup or water. It comes in all the types I explained above plus more. It's very convenient and timesaving, so if you're looking for the simplest way to make dashi, it's definitely worth looking into.

TEMPURAKO (TEMPURA FLOUR)

Making your own tempura batter isn't difficult (see page 208), but this makes it even simpler. All you do is mix it into cold water and the batter is ready to go. Great to have if you like to make tempura often. Look for it in the flour and panko section at Asian grocery stores.

Sauce Recipes

Whether you like to brush some traditional nikiri shoyu onto your nigiri or dip your roll with spicy mayo, sauces can make a big difference. Below are some common sauces that are used for sushi, but you can use them for so many other types of dishes as well.

SPICY MAYO

Using spicy mayo for sushi has become extremely popular throughout the years, especially in the United States. So much so that you can probably find a bottle of it at your nearby grocery store. I share my personal recipe that I have used for ten-plus years. For any of my past clients/customers that have been asking to buy a bottle, here you go! What's great is that spicy mayo goes well with so many different types of dishes, not just sushi.

Tools/Supplies:
- Medium bowl
- Whisk
- Squeeze bottle

PRO TIP—Spicy Powder Mix, which is used in some of my recipes, is simply a mix of the three dry pepper powders listed below.

Ingredients:
- 1 tablespoon sriracha
- ½ teaspoon Tabasco (ideally Habanero flavor)
- ½ tablespoon fine gochugaru (Korean red pepper powder)
- 1 teaspoon cayenne pepper powder
- 1 teaspoon chili powder
- 1 tube Kewpie mayo (17.64 oz, 500g; yes, it must be Kewpie)

Instructions:
1. Mix sriracha, Tabasco, gochugaru, cayenne pepper, and chili powder in a medium bowl.
2. Add Kewpie mayo and whisk together until fully combined.
3. Transfer to a squeeze bottle or jar and store in the refrigerator.

This spicy mayo can last a couple months in the refrigerator as long as it's in an airtight bottle. You can cut the recipe in half to make smaller batches, but you might not want to! Try it with some of your favorite dishes. It can go well with fried chicken, French fries, calamari (anything deep-fried really), sandwiches, salads, the list goes on. Enjoy!

UNAGI SAUCE (EEL SAUCE)

First and foremost, this is not a sauce made from eels. I get asked this quite a bit and it's a fair question since it's called eel sauce, but no, not made from eels. Unagi sauce or "unagi no tare" is a Japanese BBQ sauce that's used when cooking eel. It's soy sauce–based and has a thick consistency, very similar to teriyaki sauce. It's sweet, savory, and packed with umami, which makes it perfect not just for unagi but a lot of Japanese dishes. You can find a bottle at your local Asian store or follow my recipe below. Take note, chicken stock is not traditionally used, but it adds more depth to the flavor; this is an optional ingredient that you can leave out.

Tools/Supplies:
- Saucepan
- Whisk
- Squeeze bottle

Ingredients:
- ¼ cup mirin
- 1 tablespoon sake
- 3 tablespoon sugar
- 1 tablespoon chicken stock
- ¼ cup soy sauce

Instructions:
1. Add mirin, sake, sugar, and chicken stock to a saucepan over medium heat. Whisk until the sugar dissolves.
2. Add soy sauce and bring to boil. As soon as it boils, turn down heat to low and simmer for 10 to 15 minutes.
3. Let cool to room temperature (sauce will thicken as it cools down).
4. Place in an airtight container and keep in refrigerator. Unagi sauce will last up to 3 months.

NIKIRI SHOYU

Pronounced "nikiri-joyu" in Japanese, this style of soy sauce is a reduced and sweetened version of the regular soy sauce we all know. It's often brushed onto nigiri right before serving so that there's no need to "alter" the taste of that perfect piece. Every chef has their own recipe, but for the most part it consists of soy sauce, mirin, and sake. The recipe I'm going to share with you is easy to make and great for sashimi and any type of sushi.

Tools/Supplies:
- Small saucepan
- Strainer
- Cheesecloth or paper towel

Ingredients:
- ½ cup mirin
- ¼ cup sake
- 1 cup soy sauce
- 1 cup katsuobushi (dried bonito flakes)

Instructions:
1. Add mirin and sake into a small saucepan and bring to a boil over medium-high heat. Let it boil for about 10 to 15 seconds to eliminate the alcohol.
2. Add soy sauce and wait till the sauce is right about to boil (the edges should be bubbling) and then stop the heat.
3. Add katsuobushi and set aside for 10 to 15 minutes.
4. Layer a strainer using a cheesecloth or paper towel and strain the shoyu.

Vegetables and Other Fresh Ingredients

"Feeding your kiddo vegetables have never been so easy!" This is what we tell our friends as our three-year-old scarfs down an entire Caterpillar Roll! I mean, what's not to like? Adding vegetables in sushi not only gives it great flavor and texture, but it brings in some amazing color. In this section, I'll go over some common vegetables and other ingredients that go well in sushi. I will also be reviewing some basic techniques on cutting vegetables for sushi. A lot of traditional cutting techniques require precision. This is a great way to hone your knife skills, but please work at your own comfort level.

AVOCADO

It wasn't until sushi came over to the United States that avocados started to be used as a sushi ingredient. Now, it's one of the most popular ingredients in all types of sushi. Its smooth, creamy texture and buttery taste makes it a great complement to a variety of fish. It also makes a fine pairing with the umami of soy sauce or ponzu.

When picking out avocados, try applying gentle pressure to feel the overall softness. Ripe and ready-to-eat avocados will feel lightly soft but not mushy, and it shouldn't leave any indentations. The outer color will be more black than green while the inside will be that nice rich green.

Throughout the many sushi lessons I've given in the past decade, folks have watched me cut an avocado and wanted an avocado-cutting lesson within the sushi-making lesson. Some people may cut it in halves, quarters, or use a butter knife to make slits in it. Regardless of which method you use, the result needs to be slices that are about ¼ to ⅜ inch in thickness. If you have a favorite method that you already use, then go ahead and skip these steps below.

Tools/Supplies:
- Cutting board
- Sharp knife
- Clean damp towel

CUTTING AVOCADOS FOR SUSHI ROLLS (INSIDE)

1. Start by inserting your knife lengthwise into the avocado (start toward the middle or heel of the blade) and slowly spin the avocado full circle. You should feel the blade touching the seed in the middle.

2. Remove the seed by carefully inserting the heel and pulling it out in a twisting motion.

3. Place the flat side down onto the cutting board and cut lengthwise in half.

4. Peel the skin. Cutting it into quarters like this will allow the skin to peel off easier.

PRO TIP—Avocados change color quickly, especially if they're overripe, so save them for last. If not using right away, wrap with plastic and keep it in the refrigerator till ready to use.

5. Cut each quarter avocado into ⅜-inch-thick slices. You can cut straight down or at an angle like I am here.

CUTTING AVOCADOS FOR TOP OF ROLLS

For entire roll (Caterpillar Roll)

1. Take half of an avocado (peeled) and lay it with flat-side down.

2. Starting from the right (opposite if you're left-handed) make ⅛-inch-thick slices crosswise. Leave each slice in place after each cut.

NOTE—For rolls with partial avocado topping (Rainbow roll, Dragon roll), follow the same steps as for the Caterpillar Roll but stop after about six to eight slices.

CUCUMBER

Not all cucumbers are created equal. Standard cucumbers like hothouse cucumbers tend to be more bitter, have thicker skin, have a lot of seeds, and most importantly are very watery. Use either English, Japanese, or Persian cucumbers. Stick to my suggested types, as you don't want a soggy sushi. When selecting your cucumbers, try to find the straightest ones.

Tools/Supplies:
- Cutting board
- Sharp knife
- Clean damp towel

CUTTING CUCUMBERS FOR SUSHI ROLLS

I demonstrate two different methods below using English cucumbers. There is no right or wrong method, just preference on how you would like the texture of your cucumbers and overall sushi you are trying to make. If you can, try both ways to see what you like the best.

Method 1—This method is the easiest way to cut cucumbers for sushi. Each piece is thicker, so it'll give your rolls more of a "crunch-like" texture.

1. Wash the cucumber under cold water and pat dry with a paper towel. Cut the tip off of one end and cut cucumber to one nori sheet length (7 inches).

2. Now cut it lengthwise at about ⅜ to ½ inch thickness.

3. Take the strips and cut it down again to about ⅜–½-inch-thick strips. When cutting, measure from the skin side in order to leave the green color.

4. When finished, you should have about six to ten cucumber strips ready to use for rolls.

Method 2—This method is much more advanced, but it'll result in much thinner strips of cucumber, giving it a lightly crunchy texture. Called "katsuramuki," which is a technique typically used with Japanese daikon radish, we "skin" the cucumber and then slice that into thin strips (see Daikon section on page 26 for more information on katsuramuki).

> **NOTE**—You can also use a mandolin or peeler to first slice the cucumber into thin layers and then cut into thin strips. Make sure to remove the soft seeded part.

1. Cut a section of the cucumber that is straight, about 3 to 4 inches in length. Place your knife along the skin, slightly angled inward.

2. Start peeling the skin by gently inserting the blade while slowly rotating the cucumber. Work very slowly and do not force the knife; instead carefully move the blade up and down while guiding it with both thumbs

3. Continue until you get to the core of the cucumber. The seeded core can be discarded.

4. Cut the thin layer into roughly 5- to 6-inch length sections.

5. Stack the layers and slice into thin strips.

DAIKON (JAPANESE RADISH)

Daikon is a staple in Japanese cuisine and can be used in so many ways. It's much milder compared to red radishes and can have a slight sweetness to it. The most common way to use it for sushi is for a garnish called "tsuma," typically in sashimi dishes.

The daikon is first "peeled" paper thin using a technique called "katsuramuki" and then sliced into very thin, stringlike strips. It's a skill that takes hours upon hours of training to master. So much so that it's often a way for chefs to show off or prove their knife skills. Due to its complexity, most restaurants will use a tsuma cutting machine in modern days. I will go over the basic process here, but please note that this is a very advanced technique, and you need to have a certain level of knife skills in order to do it properly. You'll also want a very sharp knife, preferably something like an usuba-bocho (Japanese thin vegetable knife), gyuto (Japanese chef knife), or whatever you're most comfortable with (I use my sujihiki for this demonstration).

> **NOTE**—If you want to try katsuramuki, I recommend practicing with a cucumber first. Cucumbers are much softer and easier to peel. Follow the directions on Method 2 in the cucumber section of this chapter.

Tools/Supplies:
- Cutting board
- Sharp knife
- Clean damp towel
- Bowl for ice water

1. Cut a block of daikon that is roughly 3 to 4 inches in length. The more cylindrical, the easier it'll be to peel.

2. Place your knife along the skin, slightly angled inward. Peel the outer layer by rotating the daikon while carefully moving your blade up and down. This is the same motion you'll be using to peel the inner part.

3. Discard the outer skin.

4. Start peeling the daikon using the same motion as when you peeled the outer skin. You want to guide the knife right under your thumbs while rotating the daikon.

5. Continue to work very slowly and do not force the knife; instead carefully move the blade up and down while the thumbs guide it. This controls the thickness (or more so "thin-ness") of the layer.

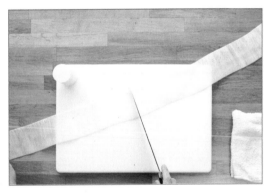

6. After you have the desired amount peeled, divide the sheet into roughly 10- to 12-inch-long sheets.

7. Roll the sheets up one at a time and lay them on the cutting board.

8. Slice the roll crosswise as thin as you can. Do this for the rest of the sheets.

9. The result should be long, fine noodle-like strips. Leave it in ice water so it stays nice and crisp until ready to use.

Katsuramuki can be used for other vegetables such as cucumbers and carrots as well. Like anything, practice makes perfect, and this takes a tremendous amount of practice. So, if you really want to master this skill, keep at it and don't give up!

NEGI (GREEN ONION)

Green onions are typically sliced very thin and then added to toro or hamachi, which becomes negitoro and negihama, respectively. But you can also cut it into thin strips and use it for rolls and hand rolls. Negi goes well with a variety of sushi and pairs especially well with fattier fish. If you intend to use it for negitoro, negihama, or any other mix, follow these steps:

Tools/Supplies:
- Cutting board
- Sharp knife
- Clean damp towel

1. Cut approximately ¼ inch off the bottom roots. Wash and remove any bad layers and remove any bad tips. Pat dry with paper towels and lay horizontally on cutting board.

2. Starting from the green end, cut crosswise as thin as possible.

PRO TIP—If you have a knife with a long blade, you may find it easier to use the bottom half of your blade to cut while the tip stays on the cutting board. You want to use sort of a circular rocking motion while the blade slices cleanly rather than tearing through. You can tell if it's tearing usually by the "crunching" sound it makes. With your other hand, make sure to always keep your knuckles forward and never raise the blade above your knuckles.

3. Continue until you have the desired amount.

For thin strips to use for rolls, follow step 1 above and then:

1. Cut green onion into roughly 3 inches in length.
2. Cut each piece lengthwise again into thin strips. You can mix the white area in as well.

CARROT

Though traditionally used more for garnish, carrots can be a great ingredient inside sushi rolls as well. As a garnish, follow the same directions for katsuramuki in the daikon section of this chapter (page 26). If you're planning to put them inside your sushi, follow these steps:

Tools/Supplies:
- Vegetable peeler
- Cutting board
- Sharp knife
- Clean damp towel

1. Peel the carrot and wash.
2. Cut the tip off both ends.
3. Cut the carrot into 3½-inch lengths.
4. Cut it in half lengthwise.
5. Place the wider side down so that it's stable and cut slices lengthwise roughly ⅛ to ¼ inch thick. Do this for both halves.
6. Julienne cut the carrots about ⅛ to ¼ inch thick.
7. Boil water in a pot and add a pinch of salt. Blanch the carrot sticks for 2 minutes. After you have the desired doneness, take it out and dump it into an ice bath to stop the cooking. After it's cooled, pat dry and it's ready to use.

JALAPEÑO

These spicy little peppers are a great way to add some heat to your sushi rolls. Jalapeños are simple to prepare and cut for sushi, as they're usually the perfect size for rolls and hand rolls. Get the fresh ones and not the ones in the jars. Just make sure to wear gloves or wash your hands very thoroughly after working with them. Do not touch your eyes, or anywhere on your face for that matter.

- Cutting board
- Sharp knife
- Clean damp towel

1. Wash the jalapeño and pat dry with a paper towel.
2. Cut the stem end off.
3. Slice it lengthwise in half.
4. Take out the seeds and wash out the inside.
5. Cut ⅛–¼ inch thick strips lengthwise.
6. Continue until you have the desired amount.

ASPARAGUS

This can be a great addition to sushi rolls, as it's very easy to prepare, easy to find, and adds a nice texture. Asparagus can pair well in a vegetarian roll or a roll with meat, like Wagyu beef. Try to find some that are a medium thickness; roughly ⅜ inch is ideal.

Tools/Supplies:
- Cutting board
- Sharp knife
- Large skillet
- Large bowl or container for ice water
- Clean damp towel

1. Wash the asparagus.
2. Measure from the tip roughly 7 inches (longer if you want it to stick out from the roll) and cut.
3. Boil a pan of water with a pinch of salt. Make sure the pan is large enough to fit the asparagus from tip to end.
4. Once water boils, blanch the asparagus for 4 to 5 minutes (depending on the thickness).
5. While the asparagus is blanching, get an ice bath ready.
6. Take out the asparagus and immediately put into the ice bath. Let it cool for a couple minutes and then take out and air dry.

TAKUWAN (JAPANESE PICKLED RADISH)

This is Japanese daikon that's pickled. It's sweet and sour with a crunchy texture and great accompaniment with many Japanese dishes. In sushi, it's mostly used for shinkomaki, which is a hosomaki using just seaweed, sushi rice, and pickled daikon, but you can add it to other rolls as well. Most Asian markets will sell them. It usually comes either full or already cut into slices. Cutting it for sushi use is very simple. Cut the takuwan right about 7 inches in length and then cut lengthwise about ⅜ inch wide. Take that strip and cut again at about ⅜ inch width.

LETTUCE

The freshness of lettuce is a nice complement to sushi. You can use it as a lettuce wrap, substituting it for nori in temaki (hand rolls). Pull apart the leaves and wash them thoroughly. Dry it with a salad spinner or paper towel. If you want to put them inside rolls, cut into thin strips, dice them up, or use a spring mix or mixed greens of your liking. Side note, BLT rolls are delicious! Iceberg, butterhead, or leaf lettuce all can work well.

SHISO (JAPANESE PERILLA LEAF)

These green (or purple) leaves can be kind of tough to find depending on where you live. They have a complex flavor reminiscent of basil or mint, maybe a hint of cilantro in there as well. It's typically used as a garnish but can pair well with a lot of fatty fish such as yellowtail, salmon, or tuna. It's also a palate cleanser similar to pickled ginger.

KAIWARE DAIKON (BABY RADISH SPROUTS)

Kaiware is baby daikon sprouts and resembles microgreens. It's commonly used as a garnish, with temaki (hand rolls) and other Japanese dishes. It has a strong radish flavor with a bit of peppery spice.

KANPYO (JAPANESE GOURD)

This is the sweet and savory brown root vegetable that comes in kanpyomaki, or sometimes in futomaki. The process to make this on your own is quite intensive, so thankfully many Asian markets sell it ready-to-go. It'll be already seasoned, have a brown color, and in plastic packs most likely in the refrigerated section.

RED RADISH

Red radish can add a slight spice and crisp texture to sushi. It is great for adding color and can also be used for garnish. Either slice them crosswise into thin circles or julienne cut them into small strips.

TAMAGO (EGG)

Eggs are used to make a Japanese-style omelet called tamagoyaki "fried egg" or atsuyaki tamago "thick fried egg." For sushi it's primarily sweetened, almost cake-like at times. The process can be very intricate and difficult unless you have experience. I share with you my recipe and steps on how to make this later (see page 214). Some Asian markets will sell frozen atsuyaki tamago.

INARI (FRIED TOFU POCKET)

Inari is fried tofu pockets that's been simmered in a soy- and dashi-based broth. When stuffed with sushi rice, you get inari sushi or inarizushi (how we call it in Japanese). You can find already seasoned ready-to-eat inari at most Asian stores, which is much simpler than making it from scratch, not to mention the unseasoned fried tofu is tougher to find. It usually comes in vacuum-sealed packs or in a can. If you would like to make your own inari, I have you covered. Look on page 194 for my recipe.

Sourcing Fish and Seafood

"Where do you get your fish?", "How fresh is the fish today?", or "Where can I buy sushi-grade fish?" are all very common questions asked of sushi chefs. As fish is one of the main ingredients when making sushi, I provide some insight on this topic to help you on your quest for good-quality fish for sushi-making.

WHAT DOES "SUSHI-GRADE" MEAN?

You might have seen or heard the terms "sushi-grade" or "sashimi-grade" here and there. But what does that really mean? To be frank, it doesn't mean as much as you think. It originally started as a marketing term to describe fish that's fresh enough to consume raw. But there's no organization that classifies the quality of fish like the USDA does for beef. The FDA issues guidelines, but again, there's no such "grading" of the fish. So, the term "sushi-grade" can be used very loosely and ultimately, it's up to the seller to decide whether it's fresh enough to consume raw. Please note, I'm not trying to scare you or deter you from consuming raw fish. Just know that there's always some level of risk and the main point to take away from this is to trust your source!

WHERE TO BUY FISH

Since it is up to the seller on whether they would consider fish "sushi-grade" or not, buying from a trusted source is important. How do you choose where to buy your fish? Below are some tips to make sure you're buying from a legitimate market.

- **Do your research.** In these modern days, practically every business can be searched on Google or Yelp, so make sure to look through the reviews! If you can't find the business online, that's probably a red flag.
- **Examine the physical space of the market.** Cleanliness and sanitary practices are obviously very important when it comes to buying any type of food, especially raw fish! Fresh fish and seafood should be displayed on ice and overall look appealing. Check to see if the display is organized. How's the color of the fish? Is there proper ice (crushed)? What's the quantity and variety? Anyone handling the fish should be following sanitary guidelines and using gloves, a hat or hairnet, an apron, etc. Use your best judgment.
- **Smell check.** All seafood markets will have a subtle smell to them, but not in a bad way. Imagine a mild and fresh ocean scent, slightly salty like you're by the sea.
- **Talk to the fishmonger.** Tell them you're planning on making sushi and eating it raw. Good markets will have qualified seafood specialists and should be able to answer any questions. Better yet, get to know them, as they could become a

Tsukiji fish market (© dreamstime.com / Ghettog76)

great resource for providing you with the freshest products as you continue your sushi-making journey.

- **Turnover.** Larger stores like Whole Foods and Costco have thousands of customers coming through daily. This means the products don't stay on the shelf for long and you have a higher chance of finding fresh fish. Also, these giant companies have strict regulations on where they're sourcing their products, so you know it's coming from a legitimate source. But note, just because it's a large grocery chain, doesn't mean the fish is of sushi quality. Again, make sure to do your due diligence.

HOW TO BUY FISH

To figure out if a fish is of "sushi quality," we'll need to dive deeper into how to pick out each type of fish. Below is a list of some of the most common seafood ingredients and how to choose the best ones.

Maguro (Tuna)

Tuna is arguably the most common and widely used fish for sushi. Whether it's bigeye, yellowfin, bluefin, albacore, or skipjack, you've probably seen it at any sushi restaurant you've been to. When buying fresh tuna by the pound, look for a deep, rich red color without too many thick grains. Note though that depending on

Sections of fresh tuna loin (© dreamstime.com / Anna Illarionova)

what part of the tuna, the color will be different. The belly side and near the collar will have more fat content and should be a lighter shade of red, but still vibrant. For example, otoro is cut from the belly side and has much more of a marble, which makes it pink in color. As tuna gets old, the color will become dull and start browning, so avoid anything that looks gray or brown. The skin (if still on) should be a nice metallic black/silver and without any damage. The meat should be smooth and firm to the touch. Ask your fishmonger to cut the bloodline and skin off if you'd like; it'll save you some of the hassle of preparing.

PRO TIP—A general rule of thumb is that frozen or previously frozen fish is safer to consume raw. By freezing fish, you kill any parasites that are possibly still living inside. In the United States, the FDA regulates this by making all retail food establishments either follow a specific freezing method or provide proof from the supplier that the fish was previously frozen. Now there are some exceptions. Aquaculture salmon (if they comply with FDA guidelines) and larger tuna species such as yellowfine, bluefin, bigeye, and albacore are exempt from this list. Though that does not mean that it's never been frozen.

Tuna for auction at Tsukiji fish market in Tokyo (© dreamstime.com / Happystock)

Frozen tuna blocks called saku is a convenient way to purchase tuna for sushi, however the quality does drop significantly compared to fresh tuna. You'll notice the color is much more uniform and brighter pink, rather than a deep red. A lot of times it's been treated to maintain that color using carbon monoxide. Not all frozen tuna saku are treated with carbon monoxide, so just be sure to read the label.

Sake (Salmon)

Salmon is another fish that is extremely popular in sushi. Because of its versatility in many different types of cuisines, it's fair to say you will be able to find good-quality salmon everywhere. When looking for salmon to consume

NOTE—Super-freezing, also known as flash freezing, is a process that can very quickly freeze fish to ultralow temperatures. We are talking about down to negative 60°F if need be. This technology maintains the quality of the fish while allowing it to last years. Even off the coasts of Japan, often the tuna is super-frozen right on the boat and then brought back to the docks. This allows shipping all around the world while keeping its premium quality. So, there is a high possibility that what we call "fresh" tuna has been frozen sometime on its journey from the ocean.

raw, stick to farm-raised versus wild caught. Farm-raised salmon can help minimize the risks of parasites tremendously. If you really like or insist on using wild-caught salmon, make sure to properly freeze it before consuming. King salmon and Scottish salmon (premium Atlantic salmon off the coast of Scotland) are my two favorite types to use with sushi, but there are plenty of other options.

Look for a nice vibrant orange color with no dark spots. Stay away from anything grayish or pale. Make sure the fillet is nicely cut meaning no tears, rips, or any meat hanging off. If it's prepackaged, then check for excess moisture by doing what I like to call a "tilt check" by tilting the package. If you see a lot of liquid, choose a different piece. When salmon is filleted into cross sections, try to find a larger piece that's taken from the middle to upper (toward the head) area. The closer you get to the tail end, the leaner and tougher the meat.

Salmon is a fish that we typically cure before using for sushi. To go through the curing process, refer to page 48.

Smoked Salmon

Widely used in the Philadelphia roll, which is also one of the more popular rolls here in the United States, and understandably so. The smoked salmon combined with the richness of cream cheese along with the freshness of cucumber is a very well-balanced combination. What makes smoked salmon so great is the long shelf life and that it's readily available

Fresh seafood on ice (© dreamstime.com / K G)

almost anywhere. It also goes well with so many other ingredients like avocados, green onions, onions, etc. When purchasing, I recommend finding unseasoned smoked salmon.

Hamachi (Yellowtail or Japanese Amberjack)

A big misconception is that hamachi is part of the tuna family, probably because the name yellowtail is like yellowfin tuna. But it's an entirely different family. Hamachi, also known as "buri" in Japan, is very commonly used not only in sushi but all different types of Japanese dishes. Hamachi has great fat content, making it rich but clean with a slight sweetness while having a smooth buttery texture. Most hamachi will be farm-raised in Japan and can be found either fresh or frozen. Look for a bright tan and pink color with no discoloration. Depending on the loin, you might see some gray/silver parts on one side; this is a thin lining right under the skin and is fine to eat. Just be sure it's not the actual skin.

Ebi (Shrimp)

Shrimp is a very convenient and versatile ingredient for sushi. You can find sushi-ready shrimp that comes in frozen packs or buy raw shrimp and boil it yourself. You obviously have more control of the quality by preparing it yourself, but it does take a bit of work. If you plan on making it yourself, purchase either fresh or frozen large (21/25 and larger) shrimp. Japanese kurumaebi would be ideal, but is very difficult to find in the United States. Therefore, you can use black tiger shrimp or other similar types. Make sure to get it with tail and shell still on.

You'll also want to pick up some small bamboo skewers. Refer to my step-by-step guide on how to prepare shrimp on page 55.

Amaebi (Sweet Shrimp)

Also known as spot prawn, this type of shrimp is one of the very few that you can eat raw. Fresh amaebi has a firm texture that's almost crunchy and has a very clean and (as the name implies) a sweet flavor to it. Most amaebi are caught and then frozen right on the dock, so look in the frozen seafood section at large Asian grocery stores. If you happen to come across live amaebi, look for a translucent color that's not turning pink; they shouldn't be curling up and there should be no black spots especially in the head area. Don't throw away the head. It's great deep-fried like a crispy shrimp cracker!

Kani (Crab)

Snow crab legs are the most popular for rolls and nigiri, while shredded crabmeat is good for gunkanmaki. The easiest and most convenient is to get cooked snow crab leg meat that's already been peeled and usually comes frozen in packs. If not, you can always crack the shells open yourself.

Kanikama (Imitation Crab)

Readily available and very convenient. Most imitation crab are made from pollock and other whitefish. Be sure to read the label if you may be allergic to certain fish. Look for the ones that are in sticks which are usually better quality than the pre-sliced ones. Kibun is a popular and good-quality brand.

Unagi (Freshwater Eel)

Though unagi is rarely served as sushi in Japan (anago or sea eel is much more popular), it is a very popular neta (sushi topping) here in the States. You can most likely find frozen unagi that has been pre-grilled and sauced at your local Asian store. I'll go over how to properly prepare (on page 70) and even make your own unagi sauce on page 18.

Ikura (Salmon Roe)

Little orange jewels of the sea. A bit salty, fishy, subtly sweet, and packed with umami. They pop in your mouth, which can almost be somewhat addicting. We usually serve this as gunkanmaki, maybe alongside some sliced cucumbers. Or they can be used as tiny garnishes for other types of sushi. You can find these at your local Asian seafood markets, and some online seafood shops may carry them. Look for a bright orange/red color that has a shine, and stay away from dark brown or anything that has lost its hue. Ikura will get slimy and almost stringy when it becomes old; stay away from anything that has a lot of liquid buildup or just looks gooey.

Tobiko (Flying Fish Roe)

These tiny eggs are like a party in your mouth. They are soft, crunchy, sweet, and slightly salty all at the same time. They add a great texture to sushi rolls and a lot of color. Traditionally, they are a red-orange color. Now you can find them in a variety of colors infused with different flavors such as green (wasabi), black (squid ink), or yellow (yuzu).

Masago (Smelt Roe)

Very similar to tobiko but a tad smaller. To be precise, they're eggs from capelin fish (which is in the smelt family). The flavor profile is almost the same as tobiko but less crunchy.

Uni (Sea Urchin)

I give credit to the first person who tried eating these hard-shell spiky creatures. But thankfully so, because the inside is full of delicate, edible meat that's rich, buttery, sweet, and briny. It's an acquired taste, and I only recommend it if you know they are fresh. They should have a rich orange or yellow color with each piece firm and intact. Old uni will start to lose its color, leak liquid, and become more paste-like. To harvest and clean uni is intensely laborious, which is why typically they can be a bit pricey.

Fish and Seafood Preparation

Preparation is key when it comes to sushi and is often the most intimidating part, especially when it comes to the fish. In this section, I'll be going over how to prepare tuna, salmon, yellowtail, and shrimp, which I like to call the "four main seafood" in beginners' sushi. These four ingredients are readily available for the most part and are extremely versatile. I also add in a couple of other fish, as I use these in some of the recipes in this book. Once the prep is finished, we'll move on to how to cut the fish for sushi and sashimi.

BREAKING DOWN MAGURO (TUNA) INTO SAKU BLOCKS

Depending on the size and the type of maguro you have, you'll either have to break it down or it might already be ready to cut for sashimi/nigiri. If you did purchase a larger amount, then you'll want to learn how to properly cut it into saku (fillet) blocks prior to cutting it for sushi. I "break it down" for you (pun intended) step by step below.

Tools/Supplies:
- Large cutting board
- Sharp knife (preferably with a longer blade)
- Clean damp towel
- Tray or large pan
- Small bowl
- Spoon

1. Wipe the maguro down gently with a clean paper towel and ensure you have a clean working area. Have a clean tray ready as well.

2. First, we cut out the bloodline. Place the loin vertically and trim out the dark area. If you look from the side you'll see the difference in color; follow that curve and keep trimming until it's completely taken off. Discard the piece.

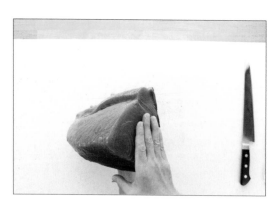

3. Next, we measure about 3 to 3½ inches from the bottom, which is roughly the width of four fingers. This is where we want to make our cut to separate the loin.

4. Lay the loin down flat with the wider end facing right (opposite if you're left-handed). Make sure the knife is parallel to the cutting board. Starting from the right side, slice straight as possible all the way to the other end. Set the saku block aside or on a tray.

5. Next, we'll cut off the skin. Lay your knife parallel and right above the skin line (tuna will be laid skin-side down). Cut into the tuna and slice across to the other side by using a sawing motion. You want the blade to stay as close to the skin as possible. Do not discard the skin.

6. Now, we'll cut the bottom part of the tuna into saku blocks. Place vertically and start from the left side (opposite if you're left-handed). The first piece might have to be cut smaller in order to make the next piece straight.

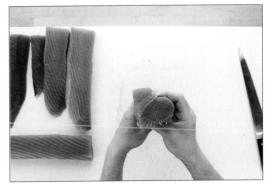

7. From here, each cut should be roughly 1- to 1½-inch thick (about two fingers' width). Cut straight down with nice long strokes. Repeat till you have a few inches left (2 to 3 saku blocks usually).

8. When you get to about the last few inches, there's a large fiber that runs diagonally across. This area is very chewy and difficult to eat, so we want to cut it out.

9. Rather than cutting straight down, insert the knife diagonally and follow the fiber as you take off the top piece.

10. Next, cut out the fiber area by cutting diagonally along the fiber line, but this time following the bottom part of it. Do not discard.

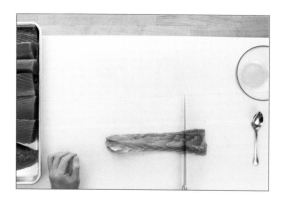

11. We don't want anything to go to waste, so we're going to scrape the meat off this fiber area with a spoon. Loosen up the meat first by hitting it with the back of our knife. Use a chopping motion, not too much force but enough to break up the meat.

12. Then we'll grab our spoon and start scraping off the meat. This can be used for rolls, gunkanmaki, or a spicy tuna mix (see page 108). Place the scraped meat in a bowl and discard the fibers.

13. We also want to scrape the meat off the skin. Use the same spoon and take off the meat by following the grain. Add the meat to the bowl and discard the skin.

14. That's pretty much it. Great job! Be sure to trim off any discolored or damaged areas of the meat. If you plan to store it for later use, follow the steps in the Storing Fish section later in this chapter (see page 63).

> NOTE—The top section that was cut off first may need to be cut down more depending on the size of the tuna. If so, you can slice it in half either straight down or at an angle.

SAKE (SALMON)

There are a couple different ways we can break down salmon and it all depends on how you purchase it. If you have a full fillet, meaning an entire side of the fish, then we'll section it into smaller fillets so it's easier to slice our sashimi and nigiri pieces. If you have a fillet cut into a cross section (see Method 2 on page 47), then you can skip the next couple steps and go straight to the curing process.

CUTTING A FULL FILLET

Before we start cutting our fillet, let me go over the basic sections of the salmon. You can see this in step 3 at the top of page 47. Starting from the top left piece going clockwise: back tail, back head, belly head, and belly tail. The flavor and texture of the salmon will be quite different depending on which section you're eating. The belly side (known as harasu) will always have more fat content and is more tender compared to the back side, which is leaner. The tail end is much leaner and often tougher, which isn't ideal for sushi. It can still be used, but I personally like to cook it instead. The ideal section for sushi and sashimi is from the middle area and up. If you like fatty and buttery pieces, then aim for the belly side. Leaner meat, then the upper back area is best.

I'm assuming that most of you probably aren't breaking down an entire salmon, so the head, fins, and bones are most likely all taken out. If you're able to, try to find salmon with the skin still on. The skin gives extra protection for when we freeze it and you can use the skin to make a delicious Salmon Skin Roll (see page 117).

There are two main ways to break down salmon. Method 1 is to break the salmon down into four sections and method 2 is to cut the entire fillet into smaller sections crosswise. There's no right or wrong with which method you choose. If you're planning on making different types of sushi, I recommend method 1. There's a lot more versatility on the way we can cut, which gives us more options on how to use the salmon. I mean, you bought a whole salmon, so I assume you're planning on making a decent amount of sushi, right?

Tools/Supplies:

- Large cutting board
- Sharp knife
- Clean damp towel
- Tray or large pan

Method 1 (Four sections)—The first method is breaking down the salmon into four sections: back head, back tail, belly head, and belly tail. This method is great if you plan to use a lot of salmon at once since each piece will be larger.

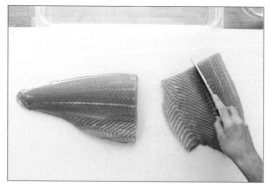

1. Place your salmon skin-side down and simply cut it in half, crosswise. You should have two pieces.

2. Next, we'll take each fillet and cut those in half, lengthwise. Follow the white line right down the center. You will end up with four pieces.

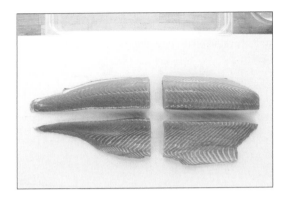

3. That's it, simple as that! If you want to cut them down smaller you can. It might be more practical depending on how much salmon you use at a time.

Method 2 (cross sections)—In this method we'll cut the entire fillet into smaller sections cross-wise, like what you typically see at grocery stores. This is good if you don't want to use too much at a time, but it does limit the way we can cut for sushi compared to the previous method.

1. Place salmon with the skin-side down. Starting from the head end, measure roughly 3 inches (about four fingers' width) and cut straight across. The first piece will not be even since the end is not straight (this still can be used for sushi).

2. Measure another four fingers from the previous cut and cut straight across again.

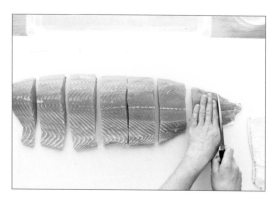 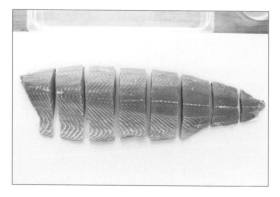

3. Continue cutting sections until you reach the tail end.

4. When finished you should have about six to eight pieces.

CURING SALMON

Curing salmon brings out better flavor and texture along with helping preserve the overall freshness. It's typically cured with salt or vinegar or a combination of both. Each chef might have their own variation. I've seen some chefs use sugar while some don't cure it at all. What I like to do and recommend is a simple salt cure for 25 minutes.

Tools/Supplies/Ingredients:
- Large cutting board or working area
- Tray or large pan (with some depth)
- Kosher salt
- Paper towel (or clean kitchen towels)

1. Sprinkle some kosher salt on the bottom of the tray and even it out.

2. Lay out the salmon fillets with the skin-side down.

 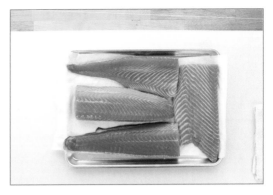

3. Generously sprinkle salt from the top so that each piece is covered, including the sides. Wrap with plastic wrap and leave in the refrigerator for 25 minutes. Don't forget to set a timer.

4. After 25 minutes, wash the salt off with cold running water. Use low water pressure to prevent any damage to the fillets. Place fillets on a paper towel–lined tray.

5. Pat dry from the top with a paper towel and we're finished! From here you can freeze it for later use or start using it right away depending on the type of salmon (see page 37—sourcing fish). If you plan to store it for later use, follow the steps in the Storing Fish section later in this chapter (see page 63).

HAMACHI (YELLOWTAIL)

Not quite as common as tuna and salmon, hamachi is still a very popular sushi neta (topping) and can be found at many seafood markets or Asian grocery stores. Fresh or frozen, you'll most likely find a loin that has been broken down already, meaning no head, fins, or bones. It's possible that they'll leave the skin on, which we can cut off. You might notice that there's two different types of loin, back side and belly side. The back side is darker in color and a lot more even-shaped through-out the loin. The belly side usually has a lighter tone and is more of a triangular shape. If you like rich, fatty, and more buttery texture, then go with the belly side. If you prefer a leaner taste, then go with the back loin.

BACK LOIN

The back loin tends to be bigger and thicker than the belly side. You should notice that there are two colors, an opaque pink and ivory. The pinkish part is the bloodline and unlike in large tunas, is fully edible. In fact in Japan, it's typically left on, but a lot of restaurants here in the United States will trim it off completely because customers confuse it for a bad-quality fish. This area is very flavorful and adds to the richness of hamachi. It is also a good indicator of how fresh the fish is, mainly by looking at its color. But if you feel more comfortable trimming it off, that is fine too. Of course, if it's discolored, damaged, or just doesn't look right, then make sure to cut it off. Use your best judgment.

Tools/Supplies:
- Large cutting board
- Sharp knife
- Clean damp towel
- Tray or large pan (optional)

1. The back loin is typically too thick to use as is (unless it's a very small hamachi), so we need to cut a layer off the top and make two separate fillets. Lay the Hamachi skin-side down and head end to the right (opposite if you're left-handed).

2. Leaving about 1½ inch on the bottom, insert the blade and cut parallel all the way across to the tail end. This will leave you with a smaller top piece and a larger bottom piece.

3. Remove the skin (see page 54) and trim any dark spots, sinew, or excess fat.

BELLY LOIN

The belly side is where you can get those rich, buttery, high-fat content pieces that's full of umami. It's usually the prized and most sought-out part of the fish (think otoro for bluefin tuna). It can be great when slightly torched or seared, which brings out even more flavor from the oils. It's best used for nigiri and sashimi, though you can use it for any type of rolls as well.

Tools/Supplies:
- Large cutting board
- Sharp knife
- Clean damp towel
- Fish bone tweezer (optional)
- Tray or large pan (optional)

1. The belly loin is going to be triangular, wider toward the head and narrower closer to the tail. We first need to divide this into two fillets by cutting lengthwise and parallel to the straight end. Leave about 2 to 3 inches on the straight side and cut straight through.

2. There's a small bone located on the head end of the small fillet. Take it out using fish bone tweezers or you can make a small cut around the bone and take it out by hand.

3. Depending on the size of the hamachi, the larger fillet may be too thick and is inconvenient to cut for sushi. Take off a layer from the top by measuring about 1½ inches from the skin side. Keeping the blade parallel to the cutting surface, cut all the way from the head to tail end.

4. Trim off any tough sinew or excess fat and discard.

NOTE—the bottom belly piece often has some lining still intact, which needs to be taken off. This can be done in the beginning or at the end.

REMOVING THE SKIN

There's a unique way of skinning fish like hamachi and salmon. It will take some practice (and a very sharp knife), but you can do it! You can simply just cut it off, but there's a very thin layer right under the skin that's full of healthy fat and nutrients that we don't want to go to waste. Salmon skin can be an exception though, since some meat left on the skin makes for better salmon skin rolls (see page 117). I use hamachi as an example below, but the method is the same for other types of fish.

Tools/Supplies:
- Large cutting board
- Sharp knife
- Clean damp towel
- Paper towel (optional)

1. Lay the fish with the head to the right and tail to the left (opposite if left-handed). Start by inserting the tip of the blade about ½ to 1 inch from the tail end, facing away from your guide hand. The blade should be touching the skin of the fish but not cutting through it.

2. Using a towel or paper towel, hold the end of the tail with your other hand to prevent any slipping. Flatten the angle of the blade nearly parallel to the cutting board and slide it down.

3. While pulling on the skin, simultaneously wiggle the blade through to the other end, keeping it as close to the skin as possible.

4. Flip it over; there should be a shiny silvery layer still left on the fillet. Trim off any remaining skin if needed.

EBI (SHRIMP)

The term "ebi" is a Japanese word that represents shrimp, prawn, lobster, and crayfish. There are many types of ebi that can be used for sushi. The most common type used in Japan is called the kurumaebi or Japanese tiger prawn. These are difficult to come by in the United States, so most restaurants will use black tiger shrimp or something very similar. In the steps below we'll go through how to prepare shrimp for sushi use.

Tools/Supplies:
- Cutting board
- Knife
- Bamboo skewers
- Pot for boiling water (large enough to fit the skewered ebi)
- Bowl or container for ice bath
- Tongs or chopsticks

Ingredients:
- Large black tiger shrimp or similar type (fresh/live is best; if frozen ensure the tail and shell is still on. Size is dependent on your preference, but don't get anything smaller than 21/25 size. I like to use 16/20.)
- 1 teaspoon salt

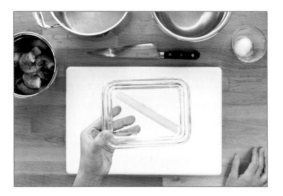

1. Soak bamboo skewers in water for a few minutes. This makes it easier to skewer the ebi.

2. With your nondominant hand, hold the ebi straight with the belly side up and tail end pointed away from you.

3. Insert the skewer from the head end (bottom), right under the shell of the belly.

4. While keeping the ebi as straight as possible, slowly insert the skewer until the tip reaches the tail. The ebi should stay straight and secured onto the skewer when finished.

5. Repeat for the rest of the ebi.

6. Bring a pot (large enough to fit the skewered ebi) of water to a boil. Add the teaspoon of salt.

7. Once the water is boiling, put in the skewered ebi. You should see the color change almost immediately. Cook for about 2 to 2½ minutes (time depends on size of ebi). Make sure to set a timer! Get the ice bath ready at this time.

8. After the time is up, quickly check the ebi to make sure it's done. The shell should be a bright orange and the inside meat will be white. You'll also feel that it's firmer now that it's been cooked.

9. Take out all the ebi and dunk it in the ice bath immediately. This is to stop the ebi from overcooking. Let cool in the ice bath for at least a couple minutes.

10. After the ebi has cooled, hold the ebi with a semi-firm grip and pull the skewer out. It may help to twist the skewer while you pull. Repeat for remaining ebi.

11. Peel the shell starting from the head, working your way to the tail.

12. Optional step—I like to take the stinger off as well (been poked with it too many times) but try not to rip the tail off.

13. Sometimes there's a small clear piece that's connected to the tail that should be taken off. Hold the tail carefully and pinch off the piece.

14. Now butterfly the ebi. Lay the ebi with the belly facing up and tail away from you. Align the tip of the knife at the base of the tail and carefully cut down using a small sawing motion. Keep cutting down until you can open the ebi fully. Do not cut all the way through.

15. Clean the entrails with cold water or a damp paper towel. Repeat for remaining ebi.

16. Optional step—I like to round the edge by cutting the corner off the head end of the belly side. This will help make the ebi look cleaner when you use it for sushi.

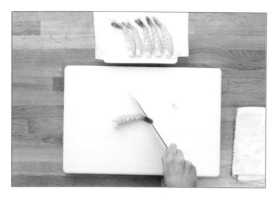

PRO TIP—If you notice that your ebi is rubbery or tough, then you most likely cooked it too long. It's very difficult to tell if the ebi is overcooked while cooking. Next time, just reduce the boiling time by 30 seconds and test it out. Practice makes perfect!

17. Trim the tail into a "V" shape. Lay the ebi on its side with the tail facing right. Cut off roughly half of the tail at an angle facing your blade to the left.

18. That is it, great job seeing it through! This can be a tedious process, but the quality is much superior to prepackaged ready-to-use ebi. Enjoy!

AMAEBI (SWEET SHRIMP)

There are a few types of ebi that can be eaten raw, amaebi being one of them. The preparation process is similar to regular ebi, but easier since you don't have to cook it! If using frozen amaebi, defrost overnight in the refrigerator. If you're in a time crunch, you can place them in a bowl of cold water for 15 to 20 minutes.

Tools/Supplies:
- Cutting board
- Knife
- Bowl of cold water (optional)

1. Separate the head from its body by gently inserting your index finger into the back neck area.

2. While holding the head in one hand, pull and twist the body off using the other.

PRO TIP—The amaebi's head or "amaebi no atama" is a great decorative piece but cannot be eaten as is. Therefore, it's typically deep-fried (sometimes grilled) and served alongside the amaebi nigiri or sashimi. It's full of savory, rich flavors, and crispy like a shrimp cracker. You can follow the same steps in the Shrimp Tempura section (page 208) to make tempura amaebi heads.

3. Peel the shell from the belly side until you reach the tail. The last shell that's connected to the tail can stay in place.

4. Next, make a cut down the center of the back to take out the entrails (some may not have).

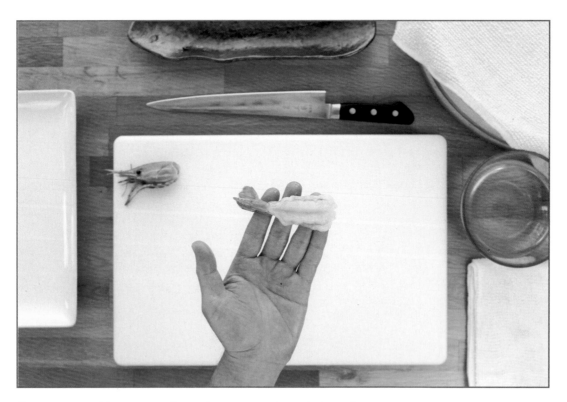

5. Rinse in cold water, pat dry with paper towels, and it's ready to go!

UNAGI (FRESHWATER EEL)

Unagi or freshwater eel has become one of the most popular sushi ingredients, especially in the United States. After talking to many customers over the years, I feel that people either really love it or are not fond of it at all. For those who don't like it, the majority is because they had it when it wasn't prepared correctly. Unagi should be broiled and served warm. When it gets cold or isn't heated up properly it becomes tough and chewy, which is not very appetizing. Heating up unagi is a very easy process that makes a world of a difference. Here is the simplest method.

1. Lightly oil a foil-lined tray (skip if using nonstick foil)
2. Place unagi onto tray. Either skin-side up or skin-side down is fine as long as the foil has been oiled.
3. Broil on high for 5 to 6 minutes.

That's it, extremely simple! Torching unagi works great as well and is actually faster than using the oven. If you own a cooking torch, place the unagi on a heat-safe plate or foil-lined tray and torch both sides for about 10 seconds each. Get too close and you'll burn it pretty quick, so control the distance and of course torch in a heat-safe environment.

STORING FISH

Properly storing and freezing seafood is critical when it comes to sushi. You spent all this time, money, and effort preparing the fish properly, so let's make sure to store it right. Most fish should be fine the next day or possibly the day after, but two days is probably max and that's assuming it's been properly refrigerated. Best is to freeze immediately after the preparation part is finished. Use your best judgment! I do not recommend freezing if you've already sliced it into sashimi or nigiri-size pieces. But rather, freeze the entire saku block right after breaking it down. It will keep much better this way.

Tools/Supplies:
*   Paper towel
*   Deli paper (optional)
*   Plastic wrap
*   Freezer-safe ziplock bag
*   Clean damp towel

FREEZING FISH

1. First, wipe off any excess moisture with a paper towel.

2. Next, using either deli paper or a paper towel (plain white preferably) and wrap the piece so that it covers it all around.

3. Then plastic wrap it twice and place in a freezer-safe ziplock bag. Don't forget to label the date. Store in freezer.

Generally, this is a good way to freeze most fish used for sushi, but some do keep better than others. For example, salmon does a great job of keeping its quality even after freezing. Tuna and hamachi are not bad, but they tend to lose their quality more. For sushi consumption, you can keep fish in the freezer up to 3 to 4 months. If kept longer you can cook it instead.

The FDA guideline is to freeze at –31°F for a minimum 15 hours (which can only be obtained by a commercial super freezer) or at –4°F for a minimum of 7 days (which most residential freezers can do). Now there are exceptions as I mentioned in the chapter on sourcing fish (tuna and farm-raised salmon). Just understand the type of fish you're working with and the risks it may involve. If you want to be on the safe side, then follow these freezing steps and plan accordingly.

When thawing, it's best to leave the fish in the refrigerator overnight. If you are pressed for time, you can thaw in cold water while keeping it in the sealed bag. Submerge the fish in a bowl of water and leave the cold water running at pencil stream so that the water is continuously refreshed.

Cutting Fish

HOW TO CUT FISH FOR SASHIMI

There are many different ways to cut sashimi. Which way you decide to cut is dependent on the type of fish, what part of the fish, and ultimately personal preference. Tender fish, like maguro (tuna), sake (salmon), and hamachi (yellowtail) are typically cut in the traditional thick-cut style called "hirazukuri." The sogizukuri or usuzukuri technique is typically for fish that are more firm such as tai (sea bream) and hirame (flounder). These firmer fish are sliced thinner to have a better texture and consistency for sashimi. In the guide below, I'll show you how to cut maguro (tuna) in the hirazukuri style, which is the most basic simple method and also very versatile.

> **NOTE**—Knowing what part of a fish is best used for sashimi is key to ensuring a good experience, so be sure to check out the Fish and Seafood Preparation chapter for my guide on the different parts of maguro, salmon, and hamachi for best results.

HIRAZUKURI (THICK-CUT) TECHNIQUE

Cutting sashimi in the hirazukuri style gives you rectangular pieces that are roughly ¼ to ½ inch thick. It's the standard for sashimi and is perfect for softer-flesh fish such as tuna, salmon, and hamachi. You want each cut to be one single stroke, therefore a longer blade such as a yanagiba or sujihiki works best (see page 5 on knives). Keep your blade clean for smoother slices. You'll also want to serve/eat the sashimi as soon as you can after cutting, so have your plate and garnishes ready to go.

Tools/Supplies:
- Cutting board
- Sharp knife (preferably with a longer blade)
- Clean damp towel

> **PRO TIP**—Maguro is a very large fish, so you'll often see fillets cut into rectangular saku blocks like this. However, if you're using a smaller fish such as hamachi (yellowtail) or saba (mackerel), place the thicker end (head) to the right and tail end to the left (opposite if you're left-handed) and with the skin side up.

1. Lay the saku (or fillet) horizontally on the cutting board. Refer to Determine Which Way to Cut on page 71.

2. Starting from the right (opposite if you're left-handed), place the heel of the blade about ¼ to ½ inch from the end of the fillet. Using the entire blade and in one stroke, pull the blade toward you while bringing the tip of the knife down to the board. Try not to use strength; let the blade do the work instead.

3. When finished with each slice, use the tip of the blade to slide the piece off to the side. Wipe the blade with a damp towel as needed.

4. Repeat until you have the desired amount of sashimi.

CUTTING HIKARIMONO (SHINY-SKINNED FISH) FOR SASHIMI

Hikarimono (shiny-skinned fish) such as saba (mackerel) and kohada (gizzard shad) are often scored with shallow slits on the skin. This gives it a better texture while also making it more visually pleasing. There are many ways to do this, but the diamond cut is one of my personal favorites, which you can see in the saba that I have cut below.

Tools/Supplies:
- Cutting board
- Sharp knife (preferably with a longer blade)
- Clean damp towel

1. Place the fillet with the skin side up. Peel the outer skin by pulling gently from one end to the other. The outer skin is edible, so this is an optional step.

2. Make light cuts at a diagonal at about ¼-inch intervals all the way across. Do not cut all the way through.

3. Rotate the fillet and repeat. Make sure the cuts are perpendicular to the original slits.

4. Now cut sashimi using the hirazukuri method explained above. For smaller fillets such as saba, make the slices at an angle rather than at 90°. This will ensure you have the right-size pieces.

5. Repeat until you have the desired amount of sashimi.

SOGIZUKURI/USUZUKURI (SHAVE-CUT OR THIN-CUT) TECHNIQUE

This style of cutting is interchangeable with sashimi and nigiri therefore, I'll introduce it here, but will go more in depth in the How to Cut Fish for Nigirizushi section in this chapter (see page 71). For sashimi, sogizukuri and usuzukuri are used for tougher flesh fish such as tai (sea bream) and hirame (flounder) where the thinner slice helps with the texture of the fish. Typically, sogizukuri slices are about ⅛ to ¼ inch thick while usuzukuri is cutting it as thin as possible (less than ⅛ inch thick).

HOW TO CUT FISH FOR ROLLS

Makimono is a very practical way of using fish, meaning you can make a lot of sushi with a small amount of fish. It allows us to use the pieces we typically can't use for sashimi or nigiri, like edge pieces, leftover scraps, or maybe an accidental tear while you were cutting sashimi. They can all be used for rolls, which helps minimize waste. I mean, sushi-grade fish isn't cheap, so we want to make the most out of it, right? If you're planning on feeding a small army, rolls will give you more bang for your buck versus only nigiri or sashimi. Something to keep in mind, if you plan on making a mix of sashimi, nigiri, and rolls, consider the order you will be making the different styles of sushi. Scraps you'll have from cutting sashimi and nigiri can add up to make quite a few rolls depending on how much sushi you're making. Just remember, once you cut fish for rolls, you can't use it to cut sashimi or nigiri, whereas fish cut for sashimi or nigiri can be used for rolls.

With that said, though, maybe you only want to make rolls or enough of it where you'll go through a full fillet. In that case, cutting fish for rolls is super simple. I go through a couple examples below using a maguro saku (fillet block) and unagi (freshwater eel). It's the same concept for other fish, so you can use these as a guideline.

CUTTING MAGURO (TUNA) FOR ROLLS

Tools/Supplies:
- Cutting board
- Sharp knife (preferably with a longer blade)
- Clean damp towel

1. Cut the saku or fillet so that its length is right around 7 inches. Lay it vertically on the cutting board and slice roughly a ½-inch-thick strip from the right side (opposite if you're left-handed).

2. Slice the strip in half lengthwise. The goal is to cut a ½-inch-by-½-inch strip that's 7 inches long. This way it will fit perfectly across the entire nori (dried seaweed) sheet when we roll.

> **NOTE**—Not all fish will be cut into rectangular saku blocks like tuna, which means you might have some irregular-shaped strips. In that case, cut and add smaller strips to make it even across the roll.

CUTTING UNAGI (FRESHWATER EEL) FOR ROLLS

Tools/Supplies:
- Cutting board
- Sharp knife (preferably with a longer blade)
- Clean damp towel

1. Open the package and lightly wipe off any excess sauce with a paper towel.

2. Cut the unagi lengthwise in half.

3. Take one side of the fillet and measure the length of one half sheet of nori (about 7 inches) and cut.

4. Now take that piece and slice it lengthwise into roughly ½-inch-wide strips.

HOW TO CUT FISH FOR NIGIRIZUSHI

Cutting fish for nigirizushi is different depending on the type of fish we're using. In the following guide I'll go over a technique called "sogizukuri" ("shave" cut), which is also a way to cut sashimi. There's also the "usuzukuri" style, which is a thinner cut of sogizukuri. This style is used mainly for sashimi, but the cutting process is practically the same, just much thinner. In the demonstrations below I'll go over cutting maguro (tuna), sake (salmon), saba (mackerel), and unagi (freshwater eel), so you have a good idea of how to cut different-sized fish. Be sure to read the Fish and Seafood Preparation chapter on page 41 to learn what part of the fish is best for nigiri.

DETERMINE WHICH WAY TO CUT

1. We always want to cut "against" the grain, meaning the lines on the tuna saku (fillet block) and the blade should make an "X." But there's more to this than simply cutting perpendicular to the lines.

   PRO TIP—The key factors when cutting fish for nigiri are the size, thickness, and cutting it properly against the grain. A sharp knife is a must too!

2. We also have to determine the natural flow of the sinew. By cutting with the flow, we minimize the meat from breaking apart, which results in a cleaner cut. But wait, I thought you just said to cut "against" the grain!? Don't panic, let me explain. The flow of the sinew isn't necessarily determined by the way the lines are showing, not from the top of the saku at least. It's related, but in this case two separate things. So not only do we have to cut *against* the grain (lines you see from the top of the saku block) but also *with* the flow. It may sound complicated, but it's actually pretty easy.

3. To determine the flow, take a look at the ends of the saku. You'll notice the grain curving one way or the other. You want to place the saku so that the lines start from the bottom and curve toward you. By placing the saku in this proper position you'll be slicing with the flow of the sinew and against the grain at the same time. Bam!

CUTTING MAGURO (TUNA) FOR NIGIRI

Tools/Supplies:
- Cutting board
- Sharp knife (preferably with a longer blade)
- Clean damp towel

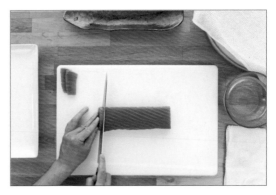

1. Place the saku horizontally on the cutting board. Start from the left end (opposite if you're left-handed) and place the heel of your blade onto the tuna. Now depending on how wide and thick your saku block is you'll adjust the blade's angle. The thinner the saku, the flatter you have to lay the knife and the narrower the saku the wider the angle you have to cut. Each piece should be about 3 inches long by 1¼-inch wide (roughly two fingers by four fingers).

2. While gently supporting the saku end with your opposite fingers, cut using the entire blade to make one clean slice. Each piece should be between ⅛ and ¼ inch in thickness. Don't use strength; let the blade do the work and also keep your knife clean in between cuts for better results. The first piece you cut off will be an end piece and can be used for rolls. Continue cutting until you have the desired amount of slices.

CUTTING SALMON FOR NIGIRI

Salmon is a very common and popular fish for sushi and can be found practically anywhere. But for that reason it can be portioned differently. A lot of times it may be already portioned out into cross sections or you may be able to find a whole fillet. Check out the prepping process in the Fish and Seafood Preparation chapter on page 45 before moving through the cutting steps below. Once the salmon is prepared properly, follow the instructions below for both types of fillets.

Tools/Supplies:
- Cutting board
- Sharp knife (preferably with a longer blade)
- Clean damp towel

CUTTING SALMON SAKU

1. Place the salmon saku horizontally on the cutting board. Make sure you're cutting against the grain and also the sinew lines on the ends are flowing toward you (see Determine Which Way to Cut on page 71).

2. Lay the knife at a slight angle (depending on the size of the saku) and place the heel of the blade onto the salmon. Support the end of the saku with your opposite fingers and make one smooth cut. The first cut will be the edge, which can be used for rolls. Repeat cuts with slices about ⅛ to ¼ inch in thickness and about 3 inches long by 1¼ inch wide (roughly two fingers by four fingers). Keep the blade clean as needed.

CUTTING SALMON FILLET (CROSS SECTION)

> **NOTE**—I wanted to show this method since a lot of stores will carry salmon that's already filleted into cross sections. You don't have too many options on how to cut this style for nigiri, which actually makes it simpler.

1. Lay the salmon fillet horizontally with the thick end to the left (opposite if left-handed). Place the fingers of your opposite hand gently to support the fillet. Cut off the first edge piece. This piece can be used for rolls.

2. Next make a cut roughly ⅛- to ¼- inch thick with one smooth motion of the blade. If the skin is still on, turn the blade sideways and cut it off the skin at the very end of the cut. You can leave more meat on the skin if you want to make salmon skin rolls (see page 117).

> **NOTE**—As you go along, you will have to adjust the angle of the blade since the thickness of the fillet changes. The thinner the fillet gets, the more you have to lay the blade at an angle and vice versa.

3. Repeat until you have the desired amount of slices.

CUTTING SABA (MACKEREL) FOR NIGIRI

Smaller fish like saba, tai (sea bream), or hirame (flounder) often use the sogizukuri technique for sashimi and nigiri. I use a saba fillet in the examples below. The concept is the same for other small fish.

Tools/Supplies:
- Cutting board
- Sharp knife (preferably with a longer blade)
- Clean damp towel

1. Optional step—There's a thin outer skin layer that can be removed from saba, but it's completely fine to leave on as well. If taking off, start from the head end and slowly peel off while you hold the fillet in place.

2. Flip the saba over so that the skin side is down. Starting from the tail end, lay the knife down about 45° and place the heel onto the fillet.

3. Using the entire blade, cut slices about ⅛- to ¼-inch thick until you have the desired amount. Remember, each piece should roughly be about two fingers wide and four fingers in length.

CUTTING UNAGI (FRESHWATER EEL) FOR NIGIRI

Cutting unagi for nigiri is simple (assuming you're not filleting live unagi).

Tools/Supplies:

- Cutting board
- Sharp knife (preferably with a longer blade)
- Clean damp towel
- Paper towel

1. Open the package and lightly wipe off any excess sauce with a paper towel.

2. Cut the unagi in half lengthwise.

3. Take one fillet at a time and place it skin-side down. You can cut either from the head or the tail end. Lay your knife about 45° and cut at a diagonal.

4. While gently supporting the unagi with your guide hand, start with the heel and cut with the entire blade. Each piece should be a diamond shape approximately 3½ inches in length (at its longest point) and 1¼ inches wide. Continue until you have the desired amount.

Sashimi

Many people outside Japan often confuse sashimi with sushi and don't really know what the difference is. The main reason for that is because people associate the term "sushi" with "raw fish," when in fact the word "sushi" represents the vinegared rice. Sashimi is actually the raw fish (or meat) on its own with no rice to accompany it. So in the most simple explanation, sushi has to use vinegared rice, whereas sashimi has no rice at all.

The word sashimi translates to "pierced meat" or "pierced body," and its origin is not fully clear. But the most common theory comes from a practice called "ikejime." In this process, fish are immediately pierced in the hindbrain with a sharp spike as soon as they're caught. This keeps the spread of lactic acid at a minimum and preserves the freshness of the fish. This method is also considered to be the fastest and most humane method of killing fish.

Because sashimi is the fish at its purest form, it has to be of the highest quality. As sushi chefs, we'll often use the best parts of the fish for sashimi, accompanied with some shredded daikon radish, shiso, wasabi, ginger, and soy sauce. It's best served at the beginning of a meal prior to eating other dishes that may affect the palate. The proper way to eat sashimi is to take a bit of wasabi with your chopsticks and place it onto the piece you're about to eat. Then lightly dip it into soy sauce and enjoy in one bite. The daikon and ginger are palate cleansers and can be eaten in between different types of fish. The shiso can be a cleanser as well or used to wrap your favorite fish for a different sashimi experience.

ASSORTED SASHIMI PLATE

Makes: 12 slices

Tools/Supplies:
- Cutting board
- Knife (preferably with a long, thin blade like a yanagiba or sujihiki; see page 5 on knives)
- Clean damp towel
- Serving plate
- Moribashi (garnishing chopsticks; optional)

Ingredients:
- ½ cup tsuma (shredded daikon radish)—for garnish (see page 26)
- 3–4 shiso leaves—for garnish
- 3–4 ounces maguro sashimi (tuna) cut hirazukuri style (see page 65)
- 3–4 ounces sake sashimi (salmon) cut hirazukuri style (see page 65)

- 3–4 ounces hamachi sashimi (yellowtail) cut hirazukuri style (see page 65)
- 3–4 ounces saba sashimi (mackerel) cut hirazukuri style (see page 67)
- ½ lemon—for lemon bowl garnish (see page 224)
- 1 tablespoon ikura (salmon roe)
- Wasabi
- Gari (pickled ginger)
- Soy sauce

1. Have all ingredients cut and prepared, including serving plates.

2. Start plating by placing some tsuma, usually toward the back of the plate.

3. Now lay a shiso leaf toward the front of the tsuma. This acts as a divider and adds some great color contrast to the plate.

4. Next, lay the maguro on the shiso leaf. Fan the slices out a bit so that it sits slightly staggered.

5. Layer the salmon next to the maguro but facing a different angle. Laying the fish in different angles can create depth and adds interest to the plate.

6. Place the remaining sashimi while using shiso leaves underneath for contrast. The lemon bowl is used to hold the ikura.

PRO TIP—Fish with bold colors such as maguro goes well toward the back of the plate since the color is so dominant. It also makes for a nice contrast with the shiso leaf and daikon. If you have different-size sashimi, place the taller pieces toward the back as well. This allows you to place smaller pieces in front without hiding it.

7. Add a little wasabi and ginger and serve with a side of soy sauce.

There's really no rule you must follow when plating sashimi. Certain fish can go well with certain ingredients, but it's mainly up to the chef's preference. Keep it simple and elegant and let the fish be the stars of the show; when you add too many garnishes it tends to become too busy, and the actual sashimi can get lost in the plate. Other than that, have fun and let the artist in you take over!

FUN FACT—You will very rarely see sashimi cut in groups of four in Japan. This is because the pronunciation of the word for the number four in Japanese, which is "shi," sounds similar to that of the Japanese word for death. Therefore, it's often seen as an unlucky number and is avoided.

Sushi Rice

Typically, when people think about sushi, the first thing that comes to mind is raw fish. However, this is a common misconception. "Sushi" in Japanese translates to "sour rice" and represents the vinegared rice instead of the raw fish. What we call sushi today is usually a combination of the sushi rice and some sort of topping, also known as "neta." But whether that's seafood or a vegetable, raw or cooked, it's all considered sushi if the vinegared rice is used. The caveat to this is sashimi, which doesn't have any rice.

Since technically it wouldn't be sushi without rice, I think it's safe to say that rice is the most important part of sushi! With that in mind, properly making sushi rice is crucial for your success in sushi-making.

In this section, I'll be going over the basic steps regarding how to cook rice on the stovetop (no rice cooker needed), making sushi rice, and sharing my 2-minute simple sushi vinegar recipe. That said, the simplest way to cook rice is to use a rice cooker so if you own one, this is the time to use it.

If you are using an electric rice cooker, a small measuring cup should have been included. This is what I call a "rice cooker cup" and is the industry standard for measuring rice worldwide. What's important to know is that it is different from the standard US cup. One rice cooker cup is 180 milliliters, while a standard US cup measures 240 milliliters. Use the chart below as a guide.

Take note, some of the recipes in this book will require a small amount of sushi rice. But when cooking sushi rice, I recommend cooking a minimum of 2 rice cooker cups' worth (which is 1½ cups or 360 milliliters) of uncooked short-grain rice. You may adjust the ratios and make a lesser amount. However, it may be difficult to control the consistency, so I typically wouldn't suggest it.

RICE			SUSHI VINEGAR INGREDIENTS NEEDED			SUSHI YIELD
UNCOOKED RICE AMOUNT	WATER AMOUNT (1:1)	COOKED RICE (YIELD)	Rice vinegar	Sugar	Salt	APPROX.
1½ cups 2 rice cooker cups 360 milliliters	1½ cups 2 rice cooker cups 360 milliliters	3⅓ cups 800 milliliters	4 tablespoons	2 tablespoons	½ tablespoon	5 rolls / 40 pieces
2¼ cups 3 rice cooker cups 540 milliliters	2¼ cups 3 rice cooker cups 540 milliliters	5 cups 1.2 liters	6 tablespoons	3 tablespoons	¾ tablespoon	8 rolls / 64 pieces
3 cups 4 rice cooker cups 720 milliliters	3 cups 4 rice cooker cups 720 milliliters	6⅔ cups 1.6 liters	8 tablespoons	4 tablespoons	1 tablespoon	11 rolls / 88 pieces

COOKING RICE

Makes: 5 cups of cooked sushi rice (approximately 8 rolls/64 pieces)

Tools/Supplies:
- Medium to large pot with a tight-fitting lid (ideally with a heavy/thick bottom and no spouts or steam holes)
- Sushi oke/hangiri (wooden sushi mixing bowl) or a large bowl (used to mix rice and vinegar)
- Shamoji (rice paddle)
- Large bowl (to wash rice in)
- Fine strainer (if using a non-mesh, make sure the holes are smaller than each rice grain)

Ingredients:
- 2¼ cups (3 rice cooker cups)—Japanese short- or medium-grain rice (see chart)
- 2¼ cups water

1. Wash the rice in a large bowl with cool running water. Gently swirl the rice around and drain the water. Repeat the washing process 4 to 5 times until the water is clear.

2. Transfer the rice into a mesh strainer and let sit for 10 minutes.

NOTE—Using the correct amount of water to cook the rice is extremely important. For sushi rice, it's a 1 to 1 ratio. So, in our case we used 2¼ cups of rice (3 rice cooker cups), so we'll use 2¼ cups (3 rice cooker cups) of water. Also, cooking rice with extra water does not make it stickier, instead it'll make it soggy and perhaps more like rice porridge.

3. After 10 minutes, transfer the rice into the medium/large pot and add the correct amount of water to the pot (see page 81). Ensure the rice is fully submerged and level. Let the rice soak for 20 to 30 minutes before cooking.

PRO TIP—If you're planning on making your own sushi vinegar, this is the perfect time to do so. Skip to the Sushi Vinegar recipe (page 86) and come back to Step 4 afterward.

4. Now it's time to cook! Place the pot over medium-high heat, close the lid, and wait for it to boil (about 4 to 5 minutes). After the water boils, turn down the heat to low and cook for 12 minutes. Make sure the lid is closed tightly and set a timer!

5. After 12 minutes, quickly open the lid to check if the water has been completely absorbed. Don't leave the lid open for long. If there is still some water, close the lid and cook for another 2 minutes. Keep cooking in additional 2-minute increments if needed. Try to leave the lid closed as much as possible.

6. Take off heat and let sit with the lid CLOSED for 10 minutes. Don't skip this step!

7. After 10 minutes the rice is done! At this point, you have plain steamed rice and you can eat it however you'd like. Next, we'll mix in the sushi vinegar, which will officially make it sushi rice.

MAKING SUSHI RICE

1. Dampen the shamoji and carve around the outer edge of the pot first to transfer cooked rice into your sushi oke. Lightly scrape off any rice that may be stuck to the bottom of the pot. Don't include any burnt or hard parts of the rice (if any).

2. Next, pour the sushi vinegar onto the rice as evenly as possible.

3. Mix the vinegar by using a "slicing" and "folding" motion. Imagine chopping with a knife but at an angle and then scoop the paddle underneath the rice and flip it over. The goal here is to evenly mix in the vinegar with the rice while breaking down any large chunks. Try to keep the rice as fluffy as possible. Continue until evenly coated and there are no chunks of rice.

4. Place a clean, damp towel over the sushi oke and let cool for 20 to 30 minutes at room temperature.

PRO TIPS—If you're using store-bought seasoned sushi vinegar, then make sure to follow the measurement directions on the label. If there are no directions, a general rule of thumb is to use equal parts vinegar to the number of (rice cooker) cups you are cooking. For example, if using 3 rice cooker cups of rice, 3 ounces of sushi vinegar should be used.

If you're using a sushi oke (hangiri), there's proper preparation and maintenance required. I go over it in the Supplies and Tools chapter, see page 11.

MAKING SUSHI VINEGAR

Sushi vinegar is made differently depending on the chef, but it will always consist of three main ingredients: rice vinegar, sugar, and salt. Some chefs may add extras such as dried konbu (kelp) or lemon, which you're more than welcome to try.

I keep my recipe (and have kept it for more than ten years) extremely simple and stick to only those three ingredients. Just because it's simple doesn't make it substandard. Making your own sushi vinegar gives you more control over the ratios used and you can create a flavor to your liking. You can make a larger batch and store in the refrigerator for later use. Make sure it's in an airtight container and it'll last a couple months at the least. You can also use the vinegar to pickle your own ginger (see page 220).

Makes: Approximately 3½ ounces (meant for 5 cups of cooked rice)

Tools/Supplies:
- Small pot (used to make sushi vinegar)
- Whisk or spoon
- Bowl or jar

Ingredients
- 6 tablespoons unseasoned rice vinegar
- 3 tablespoons white granulated sugar
- ¾ tablespoons kosher salt

1. Combine all three ingredients into a small pot and set on low heat.

2. Gently stir with a whisk or spoon until the sugar and salt fully dissolves (2 to 3 minutes). Pour into a bowl or jar and let it cool.

Makizushi (Sushi Rolls)

Makizushi means "rolled sushi" and consists of sushi rice and other ingredients wrapped together in nori (soy paper and other ingredients can be used to wrap as well). There are a few different styles of sushi rolls: hosomaki (thin roll), uramaki (inside-out roll), tatemaki (vertical roll), futomaki (big roll), and temaki (hand roll). The great part of making rolls is that after you have grasped the fundamentals of rolling, you can have fun with different ingredients and make it your way.

HOSOMAKI (THIN ROLL)

Hosomaki in Japanese translates to "thin roll," which makes sense since it normally consists of just one single ingredient. It has the nori wrapped on the outside and is usually about an inch in diameter. These types of rolls are light and often served as a snack. Although it may seem simple, making it properly can be tougher than the other types of rolls.

I'll go over the basic steps on how to make a hosomaki while covering the tekkamaki (tuna roll) recipe. It's a simple and elegant roll that only consists of three ingredients—maguro (tuna), rice, and nori (seaweed).

> **FUN FACT**—Now you may wonder why it is called tekkamaki instead of a maguro maki. There are a couple reasons for this. In the late Edo period, there were popular gambling halls called tekka-ba. The easy to eat rolls became very popular among the gamblers since they could still play their games with one hand while conveniently eating with the other. Another reason for the name comes from the rich red color of the tuna. In Japanese, "tekka" can mean "iron fire," which represents iron when it turns red-hot, hence the name "tekkamaki."

TEKKAMAKI (TUNA ROLL)

Makes: 1 roll (6 pieces)

Tools/Supplies:
- Makisu (bamboo rolling mat)
- Cutting board
- Knife
- Bowl for cold water or tezu (rice vinegar water; see page 12)
- Clean damp towel
- Serving plate

Ingredients:
- 1 half sheet nori (dried seaweed)
- ⅓ cup cooked sushi rice (about the size of a lemon; see page 81 on sushi rice)
- 2 ounces maguro (tuna; see page 69 on how to cut)
- Wasabi
- Gari (pickled ginger)
- Soy sauce

Have all ingredients cut and prepared before starting to roll.

1. Place the nori with the rough side facing up onto your makisu.

2. Lightly dampen both hands and grab the sushi rice.

3. Spread the rice as evenly as possible to the left and right edges of the nori. Leave an inch on top and ½ inch on the bottom. Try not to press and squish the rice; you want to keep it as fluffy as possible.

4. Once you have the middle section filled with rice, use your fingers to create an indentation line all the way across. This is where the maguro is going to go.

5. Lay the maguro right on top of the little creek you just made. Check the placement of your nori. We want about an inch from the bottom of the nori to the bottom of the makisu.

6. Now we start rolling! Bring the bottom of the nori up to the top of the rice. Put both thumbs under the makisu while the forefingers hold the maguro in place.

7. Gently tuck in the maguro while using your thumbs to roll the nori up. After rolling this, the rice and maguro should be tucked in and the top part of the nori should still be visible.

8. Tighten the roll by applying gentle pressure and also pulling the top end of the makisu.

9. Continue rolling by pulling the bottom end of the makisu away from you. This ensures the makisu does not get stuck inside the roll. Apply gentle pressure from the top and sides to tighten it.

10. Unroll the makisu and place your roll on the cutting board. Push in any rice that is sticking out from the ends, if needed.

11. It's time to cut! Be sure to wet the knife blade by dipping the tip of the knife into the bowl of water and letting it drip down the edge of the blade. Hosomakis are traditionally cut into six pieces. The easiest way to do this is to first cut it in half, right down the middle.

12. Then "fold" the roll so that both halves are aligned together, then cut into thirds. Keeping each piece nice and even is the key here.

13. Stand the pieces upright to plate your masterpiece! Garnish with wasabi and ginger and serve with soy sauce.

KAPPAMAKI (CUCUMBER ROLL)

Kappamaki, or just kappa for short, is another traditional hosomaki that's available at any sushi restaurant. It consists of sliced cucumber, sushi rice, seaweed, and typically some toasted sesame seeds. It's a great "entry sushi," especially for young kids.

FUN FACT—Cucumber in Japanese is "kyuri." So why is it called "kappamaki" rather than "kyuri-maki"? The story is based on an old Japanese mythological creature known as the "kappa." The kappa is an amphibious, green creature that absolutely loves to eat cucumbers. Over time, the cucumber roll started to be called kappa or kappamaki.

Makes: 1 roll (6 pieces)

Tools/Supplies:
- Makisu (bamboo rolling mat)
- Cutting board
- Knife
- Bowl for cold water or tezu (rice vinegar water; see page 12)
- Clean damp towel
- Serving plate

Ingredients:
- 1 half sheet nori (dried seaweed)
- ⅓ cup cooked sushi rice (about the size of a lemon; see page 81 on sushi rice)
- 1 cucumber stick or sliced cucumbers (see page 23 on how to cut)
- Toasted sesame seeds
- Wasabi
- Gari (pickled ginger)
- Soy sauce

Have all ingredients cut and prepared before starting to roll.

1. Place the nori with the rough side facing up onto your makisu.

2. Lightly dampen both hands and grab the sushi rice.

3. Spread the rice as evenly as possible to the left and right edges. Leave an inch on top and ½ inch on the bottom. Try not to press and squish the rice; you want to keep it as fluffy as possible.

4. Once you have the middle section filled with rice, use your fingers to create an indentation line all the way across. This is where the cucumber is going to go.

5. Lay the cucumber right on top of the little creek you just made. Check the placement of your nori. We want about an inch from the bottom of the nori to the bottom of the makisu.

6. Now we start rolling! Bring the bottom of the nori up to the top of the rice. Put both thumbs under the makisu while the forefingers hold the cucumber in place.

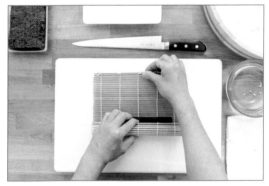

7. Gently tuck in the cucumber while using your thumbs to roll the nori up. After rolling this, the rice and cucumber should be tucked in and the top part of the nori should still be visible.

8. Tighten the roll by applying gentle pressure and also pulling the top end of the makisu.

9. Continue rolling by pulling the bottom end of the makisu away from you. This ensures the makisu does not get stuck inside the roll. Apply gentle pressure from the top and sides to tighten it.

10. Unroll the makisu and place your roll on the cutting board. Push in any rice that is sticking out from the ends, if needed.

11. It's time to cut! Be sure to wet the knife blade by dipping the tip of the knife into the bowl of water and letting it drip down the edge of the blade. Hosomakis are traditionally cut into six pieces. The easiest way to do this is to first cut it in half, right down the middle.

12. Then "fold" the roll so that both halves are aligned together then cut into thirds. Keeping each piece nice and even is the key here.

13. Stand the pieces upright to plate your masterpiece! Sprinkle some toasted sesame seeds and garnish with wasabi and ginger. Serve with soy sauce.

NEGIHAMA (YELLOWTAIL GREEN ONION ROLL)

"Negi" is green onion in Japanese and "hama" is short for hamachi (yellowtail). This combination is one of my personal favorites. The fresh green onion "cuts" the richness of the yellowtail, creating a perfect balance of flavor and texture.

Makes: 1 roll (6 pieces)

Tools/Supplies:

- Makisu (bamboo rolling mat)
- Cutting board
- Knife
- Bowl for cold water or tezu (rice vinegar water; see page 12)
- Clean damp towel
- Serving plate

Ingredients:

- ½ ounce (4 grams) negi (green onion) thinly sliced (see page 29 on how to cut)
- 2 ounces hamachi (yellowtail), minced
- 1 half sheet nori (dried seaweed)
- ⅓ cup cooked sushi rice (about the size of a lemon; see page 81 on sushi rice)
- Wasabi
- Gari (pickled ginger)
- Soy sauce

PREPARING NEGIHAMA

1. Thinly slice green onions.

2. Mince hamachi into very small chunks. The oil from the fish should come out and make it almost paste-like.

3. Mix the green onion and hamachi in a small bowl.

Have all ingredients cut and prepared before starting to roll.

1. Place the nori with the rough side facing up onto your makisu.

2. Lightly dampen both hands and grab the sushi rice.

3. Spread the rice as evenly as possible to the left and right edges. Leave an inch on top and ½ inch on the bottom. Try not to press and squish the rice, which you want to keep as fluffy as possible.

4. Once you have the middle section filled with rice, use your fingers to create an indentation line all the way across. This is where the negihama is going to go.

5. Spoon the negihama right on top of the little creek you just made. Check the placement of your nori. We want about an inch from the bottom of the nori to the bottom of the makisu.

6. Now we start rolling! Bring the bottom of the nori up to the top of the rice. Put both thumbs under the makisu while the forefingers hold the negihama in place.

7. Gently tuck in the negihama while using your thumbs to roll the nori up. After rolling this, the rice and negihama should be tucked in and the top part of the nori should still be visible.

8. Tighten the roll by applying gentle pressure and also pulling the top end of the makisu.

9. Continue rolling by pulling the bottom end of the makisu away from you. This ensures the makisu does not get stuck inside the roll. Apply gentle pressure from the top and sides to tighten it.

10. Unroll the makisu and place your roll on the cutting board. Push in any rice that is sticking out from the ends, if needed.

11. It's time to cut! Be sure to wet the knife blade by dipping the tip of the knife into the bowl of water and letting it drip down the edge of the blade. Hosomakis are traditionally cut into six pieces. The easiest way to do this is to first cut it in half, right down the middle.

12. Then "fold" the roll so that each half is aligned together then cut into thirds. Keeping each piece nice and even is the key here.

13. Stand the pieces upright to plate your masterpiece! Garnish with wasabi and ginger and serve with soy sauce.

URAMAKI (INSIDE-OUT ROLL)

The "uramaki" or inside-out roll is one of the most favored and common styles of rolls in the United States. It was created around the time sushi became popular in the country because American customers didn't particularly like the texture of the seaweed. By inverting the roll, it masked the seaweed texture. Eventually, this became the norm throughout all sushi restaurants across the country.

WRAP YOUR MAKISU (BAMBOO ROLLING MAT)

When making inside-out rolls, since the rice is on the outer layer of the roll, sushi chefs will wrap their makisu (bamboo rolling mat) with plastic wrap, so rice doesn't stick to the makisu. Follow the steps below on how to wrap your makisu before jumping into the uramaki recipes.

1. The standard plastic wrap will typically work. The plastic wrap should be at least wider than the makisu.

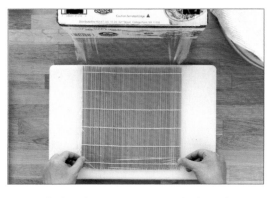

2. Pull the plastic wrap out and place the makisu on top so that the sticks are vertical to you.

3. Wrap the plastic wrap two to three times around the makisu tightly.

4. Cut the plastic wrap and fold the edges in to seal the entire makisu.

5. Cut about six to eight tiny slits into the plastic spread evenly apart (avoid cutting the strings). This prevents air bubbles from forming when we start rolling.

CALIFORNIA ROLL

The California roll is the reason the uramaki exist. It was the first inside-out roll and since its debut, it has become a globally popular roll. Sushi chefs have their own variations of this roll, but it typically consists of crab (or imitation crab), avocado, and cucumber. Its origin dates to the late 1960s. Who created this roll continues to be a debatable topic.

Makes: 1 roll (8 pieces)

Tools/Supplies:
- Makisu (bamboo rolling mat)—wrapped (see page 102 on how to wrap)
- Cutting board
- Knife
- Bowl for cold water or tezu (rice vinegar water; see page 12)

- Clean damp towel
- Serving plate

Ingredients:
- 1 half sheet of nori (dried seaweed)
- ½ cup cooked sushi rice (about the size of an apple; see page 81 on sushi rice)
- Toasted sesame seeds (optional)
- Tobiko (flying fish roe) or masago (smelt roe), both optional
- ⅛ avocado cut lengthwise (see page 20 on how to cut)
- 1 cucumber stick or sliced cucumbers (see page 23 on how to cut)
- 1 stick kanikama (imitation crab) split in half lengthwise (it's acceptable to replace with other crab options)
- Wasabi
- Gari (pickled ginger)
- Soy sauce

Have all ingredients cut and prepared before starting to roll.

1. Place the nori with the rough side up onto your makisu (plastic-wrapped).

2. Lightly dampen both hands and grab the sushi rice.

3. Spread the rice evenly onto the nori all the way to the edges.

4. Sprinkle toasted sesame seeds, tobiko, or masago on top of the rice. If using either roe, use a spoon to spread it onto the rice from one end to the other. This step is optional.

5. Flip the rice and nori over so that the nori is now facing up. Leave about an inch in between the bottom of the makisu and the bottom of the nori.

6. Place the avocado, cucumber, and crab across the center in a horizontal line.

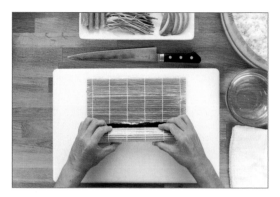

7. Now we start rolling! Bring the bottom of the nori up to the top of the ingredients. Put both thumbs under the makisu while the forefingers hold the ingredients in place.

8. Gently tuck in the ingredients while using your thumbs to roll the nori up. After rolling this, all the ingredients should be tucked in and the top part of the nori should still be visible.

9. Tighten the roll by applying gentle pressure and also pulling the top end of the makisu.

10. Continue rolling by pulling the bottom end of the makisu away from you. This ensures the makisu does not get stuck inside the roll. Apply gentle pressure from the top and sides to tighten it.

11. Unroll the makisu and place your roll on the cutting board. Align the edge of the makisu to the end of the roll and press in. Do this for both ends. This will help make the end pieces much cleaner and appealing. Set the makisu aside.

12. It's time to cut! Be sure to wet the knife blade by dipping the tip of the knife into the bowl of water and letting it drip down the edge of the blade. Uramaki is typically cut into eight pieces. The easiest way to do this is to cut it in half, right down the middle. Then cut each of those pieces in half, and then once again into halves.

13. Plate your work of art or eat it right off the cutting board (no judgment!). Garnish with wasabi and ginger and serve with soy sauce.

SPICY TUNA ROLL

The spicy tuna roll is probably the second most well-known and popular roll that can be found at any sushi restaurant (in the United States, at least). There are different variations, but typically it consists of maguro and cucumber with some sort of spice.

Makes: 1 roll (8 pieces)

Tools/Supplies:
- Makisu (bamboo rolling mat)—wrapped (see page 102 on how to wrap)
- Cutting board
- Knife
- Bowl for cold water or tezu (rice vinegar water; see page 12)
- Clean damp towel
- Serving plate

Ingredients:
- 2 ounces scraped or chopped maguro (tuna)
- ½ teaspoon spicy mayo (see page 17)
- ¼ teaspoon spicy powder mix (see page 17)
- 1 half sheet of nori (dried seaweed)
- ½ cup cooked sushi rice (about the size of an apple; see page 81 on sushi rice)
- Toasted sesame seeds (optional)
- 1 cucumber stick or sliced cucumbers (see page 23 on how to cut)
- Wasabi
- Gari (pickled ginger)
- Soy sauce

SPICY TUNA MIX

You can use any part of the tuna to make the spicy tuna mix, but it's especially a great way to use scraps or the meat we scraped off from the skin/sinew area (see page 44). If you prefer the tuna not being chopped up, then you can leave it in strips (see page 69) and add the spicy mix when you roll.

1. Chop the 2 ounces of tuna finely (skip if using scraped meat) and add it to a small bowl with spicy mayo and spicy powder mix. You can adjust the amount of spicy powder depending on your preference.

2. Mix until the tuna is evenly coated.

VARIATIONS—It's pretty common to add or substitute green onion in place of cucumber. Both vegetables give it a nice texture and complement the spicy tuna very well. Try both, and see which one you like!

Have all ingredients cut and prepared before starting to roll.

1. Place the nori with the rough side up onto your makisu (plastic wrapped).

2. Lightly dampen both hands, and grab the sushi rice.

3. Spread the rice evenly onto the nori all the way to the edges and sprinkle some toasted sesame seeds on top of the rice (optional).

4. Flip the rice and nori over so that the nori is now facing up. Leave about an inch in between the bottom of the makisu and the bottom of the nori.

5. Place the cucumber and maguro or spicy tuna mix across the center in a horizontal line. If using whole pieces of maguro, add the spicy mayo first and then lay the maguro strips on top, then sprinkle spicy powder and lastly the cucumber.

6. Now we start rolling! Bring the bottom of the nori up to the top of the ingredients. Put both thumbs under the makisu while the forefingers hold the ingredients in place.

7. Gently tuck in the ingredients while using your thumbs to roll the nori up. After rolling this, all the ingredients should be tucked in and the top part of the nori should still be visible.

8. Tighten the roll by applying gentle pressure and also pulling the top end of the makisu.

9. Continue rolling by pulling the bottom end of the makisu away from you. This ensures the makisu does not get stuck inside the roll. Apply gentle pressure from the top and sides to tighten it.

10. Unroll the makisu and place your roll on the cutting board. Align the edge of the makisu to the end of the roll and press in. Do this for both ends. This will help make the end pieces much cleaner and appealing. Set the makisu aside.

11. It's time to cut! Be sure to wet the knife blade by dipping the tip of the knife into the bowl of water and letting it drip down the edge of the blade. Uramaki is typically cut into eight pieces. The easiest way to do this is to cut it in half, right down the middle. Then cut each of those pieces in half, and then once again into halves.

12. Plate your work of art or eat it right off the cutting board (no judgment)! Garnish with wasabi and ginger and serve with soy sauce.

PHILADELPHIA (PHILLY) ROLL

The Philadelphia or "Philly" Roll is a very popular roll for sushi beginners. It consists of smoked salmon, cream cheese, and typically cucumber. It's one of the easiest rolls to make at home because the ingredients can be found at practically any grocery store.

Makes: 1 roll (8 pieces)

Tools/Supplies:
- Makisu (bamboo rolling mat)—wrapped (see page 102 on how to wrap)
- Cutting board
- Knife
- Bowl for cold water or tezu (rice vinegar water; see page 12)
- Clean damp towel
- Serving plate

Ingredients:
- 1 half sheet of nori (dried seaweed)
- ½ cup cooked sushi rice (about the size of an apple; see page 81 on sushi rice)
- Toasted sesame seeds (optional)
- 1 cucumber stick or sliced cucumbers (see page 23 on how to cut)
- 4 ounces cream cheese (cut into strips)
- 4 ounces sliced smoked salmon
- Wasabi
- Gari (pickled ginger)
- Soy sauce

> **NOTE**—Cut the cream cheese into strips. If using a standard size (Philadelphia brand) cheese, cut about ½ inch widthwise and then cut that into thirds.

Have all ingredients cut and prepared before starting to roll.

1. Place the nori with the rough side up onto your makisu (plastic wrapped).

2. After lightly dampening both hands, grab the sushi rice.

3. Spread the rice evenly onto the nori all the way to the edges and sprinkle some toasted sesame seeds on top of the rice (optional).

4. Flip the rice and nori over so that the nori is now facing up. Leave about an inch in between the bottom of the makisu and the bottom of the nori.

5. Place the cucumber, cream cheese, and smoked salmon across the center in a horizontal line.

6. Now we start rolling! Bring the bottom of the nori up to the top of the ingredients. Put both thumbs under the makisu while the forefingers hold the ingredients in place.

7. Gently tuck in the ingredients while using your thumbs to roll the nori up. After rolling this, all the ingredients should be tucked in and the top part of the nori should still be visible.

8. Tighten the roll by applying gentle pressure and also pulling the top end of the makisu.

9. Continue rolling by pulling the bottom end of the makisu away from you. This ensures the makisu does not get stuck inside the roll. Apply gentle pressure from the top and sides to tighten it.

10. Unroll the makisu and place your roll on the cutting board. Align the edge of the makisu to the end of the roll and press in. Do this for both ends. This will help make the end pieces much cleaner and appealing. Set the makisu aside.

11. It's time to cut! Be sure to wet the knife blade by dipping the tip of the knife into the bowl of water and letting it drip down the edge of the blade. Uramaki is typically cut into eight pieces. The easiest way to do this is to cut it in half, right down the middle. Then cut each of those pieces in half, and then once again into halves.

12. Plate your work of art or eat it right off the cutting board (no judgment)! Garnish with wasabi and ginger and serve with soy sauce.

> **NOTE**—Spicy mayo can be a great addition to this roll as well!

SALMON SKIN ROLL

The salmon skin roll is a great way to use every part of the salmon. When the skin is cooked properly, it turns perfectly crisp, savory, and full of that great salmon richness with a hint of smokiness. It pairs well with cucumber, avocado, tobiko (flying fish roe) or masago (smelt roe), and a bit of spicy mayo.

> **PRO TIP**—You can follow the steps in the "Removing the Skin" section in the Fish and Seafood Preparation chapter (see page 54), but I recommend leaving some extra meat on when making salmon skin rolls. You can do this by simply laying the fillet skin-side down and slide your knife across (parallel to the surface) about ⅛ inch above the skin. This will leave a little bit of the meat which gives the roll more volume and flavor.

Makes: 1 roll (8 pieces)

Tools/Supplies:
- Makisu (bamboo rolling mat)—wrapped (see page 102 on how to wrap)
- Cutting board
- Knife
- Bowl for cold water or tezu (rice vinegar water; see page 12)
- Clean damp towel
- Serving plate

Ingredients:
- 4 ounces salmon skin (about 3" × 5" pieces; see pro tip above)
- 1 half sheet of nori (dried seaweed)
- ½ cup cooked sushi rice (about the size of an apple; see page 81 on sushi rice)
- 1 tablespoon tobiko (flying fish roe) or masago (smelt roe)
- Toasted sesame seeds (optional)
- ⅛ avocado cut lengthwise (see page 20 on how to cut)
- 1 cucumber stick or sliced cucumbers (see page 23 on how to cut)
- Wasabi
- Gari (pickled ginger)
- Soy sauce
- Spicy mayo (optional, see page 17)

COOKING THE SALMON SKIN

There are three main methods to cooking the salmon skin—deep-fry, panfry, or oven bake. Deep-frying requires the most work but usually ends up the crispiest. Panfrying is fairly easy, but you still need to tend to it. Oven baking, on the other hand, is the simplest method and it comes out great! In this case, we'll be oven-roasting our salmon skin.

1. Place the rack on the lower setting and preheat the oven to 450°F. Spray or spread a thin layer of oil on a foil-lined tray and lay the salmon skin-side down. Bake for 12 to 15 minutes.

2. Once the salmon is nice and crispy, take it out of the oven and let it cool.

3. When cool enough to handle, cut it crosswise into roughly ⅜-inch-wide strips and set aside.

Have all ingredients cut and prepared before starting to roll.

1. Place the nori with the rough side up onto your makisu (plastic-wrapped).

2. Lightly dampen both hands, and grab the sushi rice.

3. Spread the rice evenly onto the nori all the way to the edges.

4. Using a spoon or your fingers, spread tobiko or masago across the rice from one edge to the other. You may replace it with toasted sesame seeds. This step is optional.

5. Flip the rice and nori over so that the nori is now facing up. Leave about an inch in between the bottom of the makisu and the bottom of the nori.

6. Place the avocado, cucumber, and roasted salmon skin across the center in a horizontal line.

7. Now we start rolling! Bring the bottom of the nori up to the top of the ingredients. Put both thumbs under the makisu while the forefingers hold the ingredients in place.

8. Gently tuck in the ingredients while using your thumbs to roll the nori up. After rolling this, all the ingredients should be tucked in and the top part of the nori should still be visible.

9. Tighten the roll by applying gentle pressure and also pulling the top end of the makisu.

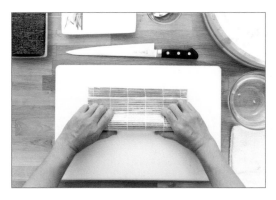

10. Continue rolling by pulling the bottom end of the makisu away from you. This ensures the makisu does not get stuck inside the roll. Apply gentle pressure from the top and sides to tighten it.

11. Unroll the makisu and place your roll on the cutting board. Align the edge of the makisu to the end of the roll and press in. Do this for both ends. This will help make the end pieces much cleaner and appealing. Set the makisu aside.

12. It's time to cut! Be sure to wet the knife blade by dipping the tip of the knife into the bowl of water and letting it drip down the edge of the blade. Uramaki is typically cut into eight pieces. The easiest way to do this is to cut it in half, right down the middle. Then cut each of those pieces in half, and then once again into halves.

13. Plate your work of art or eat it right off the cutting board (no judgment)! Garnish with wasabi and ginger and serve with soy sauce. Top with spicy mayo for a little kick!

RAINBOW ROLL

Another very popular roll that has many different variations. Typically, it has crab (or imitation crab), cucumber, and/or avocado inside with assorted fish/protein layered on top. The top layer can be whatever you like, but the most popular four are tuna, salmon, yellowtail, and shrimp. The different colors of the fish represent a rainbow, hence the name. It's the perfect roll for those who like variety or someone who wants to try different sushi conveniently in one roll.

Makes: 1 roll (8 pieces)

Tools/Supplies:
- Makisu (bamboo rolling mat)—wrapped (see page 102 on how to wrap)
- Cutting board
- Knife
- Bowl for cold water or tezu (rice vinegar water; see page 12)
- Clean damp towel
- Plastic wrap
- Serving plate

Ingredients:
- 1 half sheet of nori (dried seaweed)
- ½ cup cooked sushi rice (about the size of an apple; see page 81 on sushi rice)
- ½ avocado (for top layer and inside roll; see page 20 on how to cut)
- 1 cucumber stick or sliced cucumbers (see page 23 on how to cut)
- 1 stick kanikama (imitation crab) split in half lengthwise (it's acceptable to replace with other crab options)
- 1 slice maguro (tuna; see page 72 on how to cut for nigiri)
- 1 slice sake (salmon; see page 73 on how to cut for nigiri)
- 1 slice hamachi (yellowtail; see page 71 on how to cut for nigiri)
- 1 piece ebi (shrimp; see page 55 on how to prepare shrimp for nigiri)
- Wasabi
- Gari (pickled ginger)
- Soy sauce
- Toasted sesame seeds (optional)
- Ikura (salmon roe) for garnish (optional)

> **NOTE**—About ⅓ of the avocado needs to be sliced very thin to layer on top. This should be cut first and then use the remaining piece to cut pieces for the inside of the roll.

Have all ingredients cut and prepared before starting to roll.

1. Place the nori with the rough side up onto your makisu (plastic-wrapped).

2. Lightly dampening both hands, grab the sushi rice.

3. Spread the rice evenly onto the nori all the way to the edges.

4. Flip the rice and nori over so that the nori is now facing up. Leave about an inch in between the bottom of the makisu and the bottom of the nori.

5. Place the avocado, cucumber, and kanikama across the center in a horizontal line.

6. Now we start rolling! Bring the bottom of the nori up to the top of the ingredients. Put both thumbs under the makisu while the forefingers hold the ingredients in place.

7. Gently tuck in the ingredients while using your thumbs to roll the nori up. After rolling this, all the ingredients should be tucked in and the top part of the nori should still be visible.

8. Tighten the roll by applying gentle pressure and also pulling the top end of the makisu.

9. Continue rolling by pulling the bottom end of the makisu away from you. This ensures the makisu does not get stuck inside the roll. Apply gentle pressure from the top and sides to tighten it.

10. Unroll the makisu and place your roll on the cutting board. Align the edge of the makisu to the end of the roll and press in. Do this for both ends. This will help make the end pieces much cleaner and appealing. Set the makisu aside.

11. After finishing rolling, layer each protein on top at a slight angle. Leave a small gap in between each piece of protein.

12. Add the thin slices of avocado in between each protein. Depending on how thin you cut the avocado, you can put one to three slices down.

13. Lay a sheet of plastic wrap over the entire roll large enough so you have 4 to 5 inches of extra plastic on both top and bottom of the roll. This will help keep the plastic intact in one piece when we cut through it.

14. Shape the roll using the makisu by gently pressing the roll from all sides.

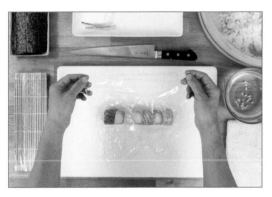

15. It's time to cut! Be sure to wet the knife blade by dipping the tip of the knife into the bowl of water and letting it drip down the edge of the blade. Leave the plastic on and cut the roll into eight pieces. The easiest way to do this is to cut it in half, right down the middle. Then cut each of those pieces into half, and then once again into halves. Do not cut through the extra plastic.

16. Reshape using the makisu if necessary and take off the plastic by pulling the part that is not cut. It should come off as one sheet.

17. Plate your work of art or eat it right off the cutting board (no judgment)! Garnish with wasabi and ginger and serve with soy sauce. Top it with some sesame seeds or ikura for more texture and flavor.

CATERPILLAR ROLL

The Caterpillar Roll and Dragon Roll are two very similar rolls and often interchanged. Typically, a Caterpillar Roll consists of unagi (freshwater eel), cucumber, and avocados layered on top, which represents a green caterpillar (the Dragon Roll recipe is right after this). You can have fun with both of these rolls and add a variation of toppings and sauces such as sesame seeds, tobiko (flying fish roe), ikura (salmon roe), unagi sauce, and spicy mayo.

Makes: 1 roll (8 pieces)

Tools/Supplies:
- Makisu (bamboo rolling mat)—wrapped (see page 102 on how to wrap)
- Cutting board
- Knife
- Bowl for cold water or tezu (rice vinegar water; see page 12)
- Clean damp towel
- Plastic wrap
- Serving plate

Ingredients:
- 1 half sheet of nori (dried seaweed)
- ½ cup cooked sushi rice (about the size of an apple; see page 81 on sushi rice)
- 1 strip broiled unagi (freshwater eel; see pages 63 and 70)
- 1 cucumber stick or sliced cucumbers (see page 23 on how to cut)
- ½ avocado—cut into thin slices (see page 22 on how to cut)
- Unagi sauce (eel sauce; see page 18)
- Toasted sesame seeds (optional)
- Tobiko (flying fish roe)—optional, for decoration
- Ikura (salmon roe)—optional, for decoration
- Kaiware (Japanese radish sprouts)—optional, for decoration
- Wasabi
- Gari (pickled ginger)
- Soy sauce

Have all ingredients cut and prepared before starting to roll.

1. Place the nori with the rough side up onto your makisu (plastic-wrapped).

2. Lightly dampening both hands, grab the sushi rice.

3. Spread the rice evenly onto the nori all the way to the edges.

4. Flip the rice and nori over so that the nori is now facing up. Leave about an inch in between the bottom of the makisu and the bottom of the nori.

5. Place the unagi and cucumber across the center in a horizontal line.

6. Now we start rolling! Bring the bottom of the nori up to the top of the ingredients. Put both thumbs under the makisu while the forefingers hold the ingredients in place.

7. Gently tuck in the ingredients while using your thumbs to roll the nori up. After rolling this, all the ingredients should be tucked in and the top part of the nori should still be visible.

8. Tighten the roll by applying gentle pressure and also pulling the top end of the makisu.

9. Continue rolling by pulling the bottom of the makisu away from you. This ensures the makisu does not get stuck inside the roll. Apply gentle pressure from the top and sides to tighten the roll.

10. Unroll the makisu and place your roll on the cutting board. Align the edge of the makisu to the end of the roll and press in. Do this for both ends. This will help make the end pieces much cleaner and appealing. Set the makisu aside.

11. Fan out the avocado slices by gently folding it down, pressing from one end of the avocado to the other. Spread it out until it's the same length as the roll.

12. Gently slide the knife under the entire spread of avocado and transfer it onto the roll. Make sure the avocado is balanced and nicely centered.

13. Lay a sheet of plastic wrap over the entire roll large enough so you have 4 to 5 inches of extra plastic on both top and bottom of the roll. This will help keep the plastic intact in one piece when we cut through it.

14. Shape the roll using the makisu by gently pressing the roll from all sides.

15. It's time to cut! Be sure to wet the knife blade by dipping the tip of the knife into the bowl of water and letting it drip down the edge of the blade. Leave the plastic on and cut the roll into eight pieces. The easiest way to do this is to cut it in half, right down the middle. Then cut each of those pieces in half, and then once again into halves. Do not cut through the extra plastic.

16. Reshape using the makisu if necessary and take off the plastic by pulling the part that is not cut. It should come off as one sheet.

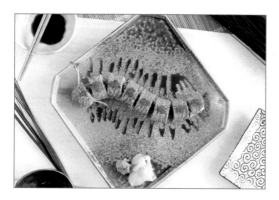

17. Have fun and get creative when plating your caterpillar roll! Drizzle unagi sauce, sprinkle sesame seeds, and add tobiko if you'd like. You can use ikura for eyes and kaiware for antennas, like in this photo or use other ingredients. Garnish with wasabi and ginger, and serve with soy sauce.

DRAGON ROLL

Very similar to the Caterpillar Roll, the Dragon Roll usually has shrimp tempura and cucumber, with layers of avocado and sometimes unagi on top, which looks like the scales of a dragon. Experiment with different toppings and garnishes such as sesame seeds, tobiko (flying fish roe), ikura (salmon roe), unagi sauce, and spicy mayo.

Makes: 1 roll (8 pieces)

Tools/Supplies:
- Makisu (bamboo rolling mat)—wrapped (see page 102 on how to wrap)
- Cutting board
- Knife
- Bowl for cold water or tezu (rice vinegar water; see page 12)
- Clean damp towel
- Plastic wrap
- Serving plate

Ingredients:
- 1 half sheet of nori (dried seaweed)
- ½ cup cooked sushi rice (about the size of an apple; see page 81 on sushi rice)
- 1 cucumber stick or sliced cucumbers (see page 23 on how to cut)
- 2 pieces of shrimp tempura (see page 208)
- 4 pieces broiled unagi (freshwater eel; see pages 63 and 76)
- ½ avocado (for top layer; see page 22 on how to cut)
- Unagi sauce (eel sauce; see page 18)
- Spicy mayo (optional, see page 17)
- Toasted sesame seeds (optional)
- Wasabi
- Gari (pickled ginger)
- Soy sauce

Have all ingredients cut and prepared before rolling.

1. Place the nori with the rough side up onto your makisu (plastic-wrapped).

2. Lightly dampening both hands, grab the sushi rice.

3. Spread the rice evenly onto the nori all the way to the edges.

4. Flip the rice and nori over so that the nori is now facing up. Leave about an inch in between the bottom of the makisu and the bottom of the nori.

5. Place the cucumber and shrimp tempura horizontally across the middle. The tails should be sticking out from both ends.

6. Now we start rolling! Bring the bottom of the nori up to the top of the ingredients. Put both thumbs under the makisu while the forefingers hold the ingredients in place.

7. Gently tuck in the ingredients while using your thumbs to roll the nori up. After rolling this, all the ingredients should be tucked in and the top part of the nori should still be visible.

8. Tighten the roll by applying gentle pressure and also pulling the top end of the makisu.

9. Continue rolling by pulling the bottom of the makisu away from you. This ensures the makisu does not get stuck inside the roll. Apply gentle pressure from the top and sides to tighten the roll.

10. Unroll the makisu and place your roll on the cutting board. Align the edge of the makisu to the end of the roll and press in. Do this for both ends. This will help make the end pieces much cleaner and appealing. Set the makisu aside.

11. Lay each piece of unagi on top of the roll, evenly spaced out.

12. Fill in the gaps with the avocado slices.

13. Lay a sheet of plastic wrap over the entire roll large enough so you have 4 to 5 inches of extra plastic on both top and bottom of the roll. This will help keep the plastic intact in one piece when we cut through it.

14. Shape the roll using the makisu by gently pressing the roll from all sides.

15. It's time to cut! Be sure to wet the knife blade by dipping the tip of the knife into the bowl of water and letting it drip down the edge of the blade. Leave the plastic on and cut the roll into eight pieces. The easiest way to do this is to cut it in half, right down the middle. Then cut each of those pieces in half, and then once again into halves. Do not cut through the extra plastic.

16. Reshape using the makisu if necessary and take off the plastic by pulling the part that is not cut. It should come off as one sheet.

17. After plating, drizzle unagi sauce and spicy mayo over the entire roll. Sprinkle sesame seeds, garnish with wasabi and ginger, and serve with soy sauce.

TATEMAKI (VERTICAL ROLL)

In this method, we rotate our seaweed so that we roll vertically rather than horizontally. This allows more room inside so we can fit more ingredients. It's ideal for larger ingredients such as shrimp tempura or soft-shell crab (for spider rolls). And it's always a fun one to make since you can add so many things inside. The concept is the exact same as the uramaki (inside-out roll) but we just rotate it 90°, which actually makes it easier to roll.

SHRIMP TEMPURA ROLL

Shrimp tempura rolls can be made in a variety of different ways, as long as it consists of tempura shrimp of course. You can make these in the traditional uramaki style, but a lot of times the shrimp is pretty thick so you can't add much more into this style of roll. So personally, I make tempura rolls by rolling it vertically and add a few more complementing ingredients to it.

Makes: 1 roll (5 pieces)

Tools/Supplies:
- Makisu (bamboo rolling mat)—wrapped (see page 102 on how to wrap)
- Cutting board
- Knife
- Bowl for cold water or tezu (rice vinegar water; see page 12)
- Clean damp towel
- Serving plate

Ingredients:
- 1 half sheet of nori (dried seaweed)
- ½ cup cooked sushi rice (about the size of an apple; see page 81 on sushi rice)
- Toasted sesame seeds (optional)
- ½ cucumber stick or sliced cucumbers (see page 23 on how to cut)
- ⅛ avocado—cut lengthwise (see page 20 on how to cut)
- 1 stick kanikama (imitation crab; it's acceptable to replace with other crab options)
- 1 piece shrimp tempura (see page 208)
- Unagi sauce (eel sauce; see page 18)
- Spicy mayo (optional, see page 17)
- Wasabi
- Gari (pickled ginger)
- Soy sauce

Have all ingredients cut and prepared before rolling.

1. Place the nori with the rough side up onto your makisu (plastic wrapped). Lay the seaweed vertically so that the short ends are laying top and bottom.

2. Lightly dampening both hands, grab the sushi rice.

3. Spread the rice evenly onto the nori all the way to the edges and sprinkle some toasted sesame seeds on top of the rice (optional).

4. Flip the rice and nori over so that the nori is now facing up. Leave about an inch in between the bottom of the makisu and the bottom of the nori.

5. Place cucumber, avocado, imitation crab, and shrimp tempura across the center in a horizontal line.

6. Now we start rolling! Bring the bottom of the nori up to the top of the ingredients. Put both thumbs under the makisu while the forefingers hold the ingredients in place.

7. Gently tuck in the ingredients while using your thumbs to roll the nori up. After rolling this, all the ingredients should be tucked in and the top part of the nori should still be visible.

8. Tighten the roll by applying gentle pressure and also pulling the top end of the makisu.

9. Continue rolling by pulling the bottom end of the makisu away from you. This ensures the makisu does not get stuck inside the roll. Apply gentle pressure from the top and sides to tighten it.

10. Unroll the makisu and place your roll on the cutting board. Align the edge of the makisu to the end of the roll and press in. Do this for both ends. This will help make the end pieces much cleaner and appealing. Set the makisu aside.

11. It's time to cut! Be sure to wet the knife blade by dipping the tip of the knife into the bowl of water and letting it drip down the edge of the blade. Since the roll is rolled vertically, it'll be shorter but thicker than the uramaki (inside-out roll). That is why we want to cut this into five pieces rather than eight.

12. After plating, drizzle both unagi sauce and spicy mayo on top. Garnish with wasabi and ginger, and serve with soy sauce.

FUTOMAKI ("BIG" ROLL)

FUTOMAKI

This is a fun one, and the name says it all! Imagine the modern-day sushi burrito but in a traditional form. The Futomaki is actually one of the oldest forms of sushi rolls and is often enjoyed at picnics and festive events in Japan. What makes it super fun is that there's really no limit to what you can put inside. There are popular ingredients, but every family has their own recipe. So use what you think would be good and have fun with it! For this guide, I'll be sharing with you what I personally like to put in our Futomaki.

Makes: 1 roll (8 pieces)

Tools/Supplies:
- Makisu (bamboo rolling mat)
- Cutting board
- Knife
- Bowl for cold water or tezu (rice vinegar water; see page 12)
- Clean damp towel
- Serving plate

Ingredients:
- 1 full sheet of nori (dried seaweed)
- 1 cup cooked sushi rice (about the size of a mango; see page 81 on sushi rice)
- 1 tablespoon tobiko (flying fish roe) or masago (smelt roe)
- 1 cucumber stick or sliced cucumbers (see page 23 how to cut)
- 7–8 pieces of braised shiitake mushroom (see page 204)
- 2 strips tamagoyaki (Japanese egg omelet; see page 214)
- 3–4 strips braised kanpyo (Japanese gourd; see page 32)
- 1 stick kanikama (imitation crab) split in half lengthwise (it's acceptable to replace with other crab options)
- 1 strip broiled unagi (freshwater eel; see pages 63 and 70)
- Wasabi
- Gari (pickled ginger)
- Soy sauce

Have all ingredients cut and prepared before starting to roll.

1. Place the full sheet of nori rough-side up on your makisu with the shorter side facing top and bottom.

2. Lightly dampening both hands, grab the sushi rice).

3. Spread the rice as evenly as possible to the left and right edges. Leave about ½ inch on the bottom and 1½ inch at the top. Try not to press and squish the rice, you want to keep it as fluffy as possible.

4. Spread the tobiko or masago onto the rice across the center horizontally (about 2 to 3 inches wide).

5. Place the cucumber, shiitake mushrooms, tamagoyaki, kanpyo, kanikama, and unagi one by one neatly in the middle of the roll. Ensure that it goes all the way across. Check the placement of your nori. We want about an inch from the bottom of the nori to the bottom of the makisu.

6. Now we start rolling! Bring the bottom of the nori up to the top part of the rice. Put both thumbs under the makisu while the forefingers hold the ingredients in place.

7. Gently tuck in the ingredients while using your thumbs to roll the nori up. After rolling this, the ingredients should be tucked in and the top part of the nori should still be visible.

8. Tighten the roll by applying gentle pressure and also pulling the top end of the makisu.

9. Continue rolling by pulling the bottom end of the makisu away from you. This ensures the makisu does not get stuck inside the roll. Apply gentle pressure from the top and sides to tighten it.

10. Unroll the makisu and place your roll on the cutting board. Align the edge of the makisu to the end of the roll and press in. Do this for both ends. This will help make the end pieces much cleaner and appealing. Set the makisu aside.

11. It's time to cut! Be sure to wet the knife blade by dipping the tip of the knife into the bowl of water and letting it drip down the edge of the blade. Futomakis are typically cut into eight pieces. The easiest way to do this is to cut it right down the middle in half. And then cut each of those pieces in half, and then once again into halves. Make sure to keep the blade clean in between cuts.

12. Plate your work of art or eat it right off the cutting board (no judgment)! Garnish with wasabi and ginger, and serve with soy sauce.

TEMAKI (HAND ROLL)

Temaki sushi (pronounced "temaki-zushi" in Japanese) means "hand-roll" and is a cone-shaped roll filled with rice and other sushi ingredients. It's often made in Japanese households and is the perfect way to have a sushi party. The rolling technique is simple, and each person rolls their own with whatever ingredients they prefer (makes it much easier for the person that's preparing everything!). In this recipe, I'll share the typical ingredients we use for our temaki parties, but there's really no right or wrong, you're free to add whatever you think will go well.

TEMAKI PARTY

Makes: 20–25 hand rolls (serves approximately 4–6 people)

Tools/Supplies:
- Cutting board
- Knife
- Bowl for cold water or tezu (rice vinegar water; see page 12)
- Clean damp towel
- Serving plates

Ingredients:
- 5 cups cooked sushi rice (see page 81 on sushi rice)
- 25 half sheets of nori (dried seaweed)
- ½ pound of maguro (tuna; see page 69 on how to cut)
- ½ pound of sake (salmon; see page 69 on how to cut)
- ½ pound of hamachi (yellowtail; see page 69 on how to cut)
- ½ pound of broiled unagi (freshwater eel; see pages 63 and 70)
- 6–8 pieces ebi (shrimp; see page 55)
- 6–8 sticks kanikama (imitation crab; it's acceptable to replace with other crab options)
- ¼ pound ikura (salmon roe)
- ¼ pound tobiko (flying fish roe) or masago (smelt roe)
- 1–2 avocados sliced for sushi rolls (see page 20 on how to cut)
- ½ cucumber sliced or sticks (see page 23 on how to cut)
- 2–3 green onions sliced into thin strips (see page 29)
- Spicy mayo (see page 17)
- Unagi sauce (eel sauce; see page 18)
- Toasted sesame seeds (optional)

- Wasabi
- Gari (pickled ginger)
- Soy sauce

Other Additional Ingredients:
- Jalapeños sliced into thin strips (see page 30 on how to cut)
- Kaiware daikon (Japanese radish sprouts; see page 32)
- Lettuce for lettuce wraps (see page 32 on how to prepare)

PREPARATION FOR TEMAKI

1. First thing we want to prepare is the sushi rice. Follow the steps in the Sushi Rice section (see page 81).
2. Prepare and cut all protein and vegetables by following the corresponding guide on each page. Fish should be cut just like for rolls but in 3- to 4-inch-long pieces. Place each ingredient separately either together on a large plate or multiple plates.
3. Set the table with all ingredients (sushi rice, protein, vegetables, nori, all condiments, chopsticks, shamoji for the rice, spoons, etc.).

HOW TO MAKE TEMAKI

1. Make sure that your hands are completely dry. Place the seaweed (horizontally) so that the left half sits on your palm. The rough side of the seaweed should be facing up. (Opposite if you're left-handed).

2. Scoop a thin layer of sushi rice onto the left side of the seaweed. You don't have to put too much where it touches the edges. Imagine a kite shape.

3. Now place the ingredients of your choice in a 45° angle across from the top left to the bottom center, right on top of the rice. In this example I will be using some unagi, cucumber, and avocado to make an unagi hand roll.

4. Next, wrap all the filling with the seaweed by taking the bottom left corner and bringing it up to the top middle. Gently fold your left hand while the right helps wrap the seaweed around.

5. Continue rolling so that the nori wraps around on itself in the shape of a cone.

6. If you like, use a couple grains of rice to hold the nori in place (or just hold it and eat it right away like I do).

PRO TIP—You can also use ¼ sheets of nori and make each roll smaller. This is the way we make ours at home. Each roll will have less fillings, but you can make more variety. Try both ways and see what you like!

7. For the unagi hand roll, drizzle some unagi sauce and sprinkle on some toasted sesame seeds and that's it! Dip it in some soy sauce and eat it right away before the seaweed gets soggy.

Nigirizushi

Nigirizushi or nigiri sushi is one of the most pure and traditional forms of sushi that dates back hundreds of years. A combination of sushi rice with a slice of raw fish (typically), hand-formed to create a perfectly balanced piece, all enjoyed in one single bite. There's just nothing like it. Although the concept is simple, it may be the toughest style of sushi to master.

Nigiri in Japanese means to grasp or grip with your hand, making the English translation for nigiri-zushi, "hand-formed sushi." And no that is not a typo, the proper way to say "nigiri-sushi" in Japanese is actually nigiri-zushi with a "z." The word "sushi" is a general term when the type of sushi is not specified. But when talking about a specific type of sushi such as nigiri-zushi, temaki-zushi, or chirashi-zushi, that "s" turns into a "z." I know, the Japanese language can get complicated!

> **FUN FACT**—I get asked about the pronunciation of the word "nigiri" by many customers. It does get butchered a lot; trust me, I've heard it all. The correct way is broken down like this:
>
> "Ni" = "knee" (don't extend the ee)
> "Gi" = pronounced "gee" like in "geese" but don't extend the "e"
> "Ri" = closer to the pronunciation of the letter "L" such as the name "Lee" (don't extend the "e" at the end)

In this section, I'll be going over the basics on how to properly make nigirizushi (or nigiri for short) using a traditional style called kotegaeshi (side-flip technique). It is the most common and widely used style, and once you get the hang of it, you can use the same technique to make almost any other nigiri.

ASSORTED NIGIRI PLATTER

Makes: 20 pieces

Tools/Supplies:
- Cutting board
- Knife
- Bowl for cold water or tezu (rice vinegar water; see page 12)

- Clean damp towel
- Serving plate
- Moribashi (garnishing chopsticks)—optional

Ingredients:
- 2 cups cooked sushi rice (see page 81 on sushi rice)
- 20 pieces of sushi neta (fish/protein) of your choice (see page 71 on how to cut)
- Wasabi
- Gari (pickled ginger)
- Soy sauce

Have all ingredients cut and prepared prior to making nigiri.

1. Wet both hands by dipping into the tezu or cold water. Make sure to spread it across both hands thoroughly. The palms should be wet and shiny but not dripping.

2. Hold the slice of fish with your nondominant hand (in my case the left). Place the fish right along the base of your finger and use your thumb to hold it there. Whichever side of the fish you want to be on top at the end needs to be placed down here.

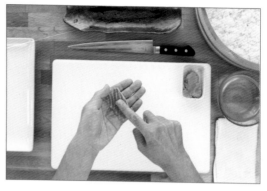

3. Make the sharidama (rice ball) with your dominant hand. Grab some rice and form it into a small ball slightly smaller than a ping pong ball. You want to lightly apply pressure while rolling the ball around in your palm but do not squeeze the rice too tight. If you want to get technical, each sharidama should be around 15 to 16 grams or about ½ ounce.

4. With the same hand that's holding the rice, use the index finger to spread some wasabi onto the fish. Skip this step if you prefer not to have wasabi.

5. Next, place the rice onto the center of the fish and using your left thumb, push a hole into the rice. This hole will help keep the rice fluffier and results in a better texture.

6. Now close the hole by gently clamping your left palm while using your right thumb and index in a pinching motion. Imagine the hole creating an air pocket inside the sharidama.

7. From here, we'll flip it over sideways by rolling it toward the tip of our fingers. This is what defines the kotegaeshi method.

8. Now the fish should be on top. From here, gently clamp the sides using our right hand while applying pressure from the top with our left thumb.

9. Then we move the nigiri back down toward the base of our fingers. When we do this, place the left thumb under the fish so that it can press on the rice.

10. Next we apply pressure by gently clamping our left hand (including the thumb) and using our right index to support the top of the nigiri. You can use one or two fingers on your right hand here.

11. Rotate the nigiri 180° and repeat step 10.

12. Turn 180° once again and repeat step 10 if necessary.

13. Clamp the sides for final shaping.

14. When finished, you should have a nice arc-shaped piece with the fish following a smooth curve. You should be able to see each grain of rice, and the sharidama loose enough but still holding its shape. When compressed too tight, the rice will become chewy similar to mochi.

15. Repeat steps for remaining pieces and garnish if you'd like.

16. Plate and serve with wasabi, ginger, and soy sauce on the side. Or I recommend brushing on some nikiri soy sauce (see page 19).

PRO TIP—Making nigirizushi has to be done quickly for a couple reasons. One, your hands dry out which causes the rice to stick, and second, the fish becomes warm if held in your hand for too long. The best way to practice is to use only rice, no neta until you get a good feel of making the sharidama (rice ball). After that, start by using ebi (shrimp). Because shrimp is cooked and not as delicate, you'll be able to keep reusing it for practice.

Gunkanmaki (Battleship Sushi)

Gunkanmaki (or gunkan for short) is a hybrid between nigirizushi and makizushi. The name implies that it's a "maki" (roll), which it is since it has seaweed wrapped around it, but it's also considered nigiri because it's "hand-formed." Each piece is made from a ball of rice, wrapped with a sheet of seaweed with room left at the top for various toppings. This oval, boat-like shape is the reason for the name "gunkan," meaning battleship or warship in Japanese. This innovative style founded decades ago allowed chefs to serve toppings that couldn't be used in regular nigiri and became extremely popular worldwide. Some well-known gunkanmaki includes ikura (salmon roe), masago (smelt roe), tobiko (flying fish roe), negitoro (fatty tuna and green onion), uni (sea urchin)—the list goes on.

Making gunkanmaki is a lot simpler compared to regular nigiri. It's easy to make it look professional without having much experience. Just be sure to have all the ingredients ready because as soon as the seaweed touches the rice it'll absorb the moisture and start to lose its crispiness. If you plan on making other types of sushi along with any gunkunmakis, be sure these are the last pieces you make prior to serving or eating.

ASSORTED GUNKANMAKI PLATE

Makes: 9 pieces

Tools/Supplies:
- Cutting board
- Knife
- Bowl for cold water or tezu (rice vinegar water; see page 12)
- Clean, damp towel
- Serving plate

Ingredients:
- 3 half sheets of nori (dried seaweed) cut for gunkanmaki
- 1 cup cooked sushi rice (see page 81 on sushi rice)
- 9 toppings of your choice (see below for topping suggestions)

- Wasabi
- Gari (pickled ginger)
- Soy sauce

GUNKANMAKI TOPPINGS

There are the traditional and popular toppings for gunkanmaki, which I'll go over here in a bit, but the beauty of this is you can practically put anything you want on there. I've seen everything from corn salad to Wagyu beef tartare, and it's pretty darn good! So experiment with what you like and have fun. Sometimes a garnish, squeeze of lemon, or slight sprinkle of salt often improves the taste from ordinary to fantastic, so get adventurous!

Ikura (salmon roe)—very popular and one of the gunkanmaki originals. It pairs very well with thinly sliced cucumber.

Tobiko (flying fish roe) or masago (smelt roe)—both very popular and standard gunkanmaki toppings. Uzura (raw quail egg yolk) is a popular combination with tobiko or masago. If using uzura, gently crack the egg and separate the yolk from the white. Then make a pocket on top of the tobiko or masago with your finger and slide the yolk on top.

Uni (sea urchin)—though I've seen uni made in a regular nigiri style, majority of the time it's served as gunkanmaki. Depending on the size of the uni, there could be one to five pieces on top. I don't really recommend adding anything to it, especially if you're able to get really fresh uni. The simple combination of fresh uni, sushi rice, and crispy nori is very hard to beat.

Negitoro (fatty tuna and green onion)—This combination is great in all different types of sushi, and gunkanmaki is definitely one of them. The fresh green onion "cuts" the richness of the fatty tuna, creating a perfect balance of flavor and texture.

Negihama (yellowtail and green onion)—very similar to negitoro, here you are using yellowtail instead of fatty tuna. Also great with all different types of sushi including gunkanmaki.

Spicy tuna—Same mix as the spicy tuna roll recipe (see page 108). This pairs nicely with some sliced green onion on top or some cucumber slices.

> **PRO TIP**—If you want a nori substitution, you can use a long thin slice of cucumber, a thin cut of salmon, or thin cut of smoked salmon.

Have all ingredients including toppings prepared prior to making the gunkanmaki.

1. Take a half sheet of seaweed and cut two strips (about ⅜-inch wide each) crosswise. Save these strips because they are used for nigiri-zushi that requires an "obi" (belt), such as tamago (Japanese egg omelet) and unagi (freshwater eel).

2. Next, cut the large piece of seaweed into three strips lengthwise. This makes the perfect size nori for gunkanmaki.

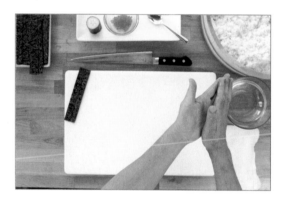

3. Wet both hands by dipping into the tezu or cold water. Make sure to spread it across both hands thoroughly. The palms should be wet and shiny but not dripping.

4. Make the sharidama (rice ball) with our dominant hand. Grab some rice and form it into a small ball about the size of a Ping-Pong ball. You want to lightly apply pressure while rolling the ball around in your palm but do not squeeze the rice too tight. The weight should be slightly more than a regular nigiri, about 18 to 20 grams.

5. From here, the steps are the same as when making regular nigiri, just without the fish. Follow steps 6 to 11 in the Nigirizushi section (page 159). The shape should be more of a log rather than a ball when you're finished. Prepare all nine pieces before we move to the next step.

6. Take each ball of rice at a time and wrap a strip of nori around it, rough side facing in. The bottom of the nori should be parallel and touching the surface.

7. Start with the rice in the center of the strip and wrap it around completely so that seaweed wraps around on itself. Fuse the overlap with a grain of rice if needed.

8. Press down gently on the rice from the top. You want it to be slightly concave so that the fillings have a spot to sit properly. Do the same for the remaining pieces. You can also add a bit of wasabi onto the rice here if you'd like.

9. Add the toppings with a spoon and you're done!

10. Plate and serve/eat immediately. Don't let gunkanmaki sit for too long; just like temaki, it's best when the seaweed is still crisp. Enjoy!

Temarizushi (Sushi Ball)

Temarizushi—or temari sushi—received its name from Japanese embroidered balls called "temari," which translates to "hand-ball." It was originally made for children's games like hacky sack. Now it's used more for decorative ornaments due to its beautiful rich color and craftsmanship.

Making this type of sushi doesn't require much experience, and you're free to use whatever ingredient you like. I'll go over the steps on how to create one and share some ideas for toppings, but feel free to venture out and experiment!

ASSORTED TEMARI PLATE

Makes: 9 pieces

Tools/Supplies:
- Cutting board
- Knife
- Bowl for cold water or tezu (rice vinegar water; see page 12)
- Clean damp towel
- Serving plate
- Plastic wrap
- Moribashi (garnishing chopsticks)—optional

Ingredients:
- 1 cup cooked sushi rice (see page 81 on sushi rice)
- 9 toppings of your choice (see page 171 for suggestions)
- Wasabi
- Gari (pickled ginger)
- Soy sauce

TEMARI TOPPINGS

Fish/protein prepared for nigiri sushi (see page 71)—When cutting fish for temari, slice it a tad thinner and about ⅔ the length of nigiri sushi pieces. Or you can slice it into smaller pieces and layer it, which adds some nice texture. Tuna, salmon, yellowtail, sea bream, shrimp, eel, are just some of the common ingredients you can use.

Cucumber—Thin sliced cucumbers in full circles, semicircles, or strips are great for temari. Combine it with a bright color fish such as tuna or salmon to make the piece pop.

Avocado—Slice thin and layer on top, similar to how it was made for the Caterpillar Roll (see page 22). It can be a topping on its own or added to any fish or protein.

Tamago (Japanese egg)—There are two styles of tamago that you can choose from. One is to make a block of tamagoyaki (see page 214) and slice thin strips from there. Second, make what's called kinshi tamago (see page 186). The bright yellow color from the egg provides a nice color contrast with the deep green/black with nori.

Red radish—Slice these up very thin and lay them down to look like flower petals. Goes well with some ikura or other types of roe on top.

Shiso leaves—Shiso has a vibrant color and pairs well with a lot of fatty fishes. You can slice it up small and use it as garnish too.

Kaiware daikon—These are great to use as garnish, adding some green color and a light kick.

Ikura (salmon roe)—Ikura is perfect for garnish, adding a bright orange color and bursts of flavor.

Tobiko (flying fish roe) or masago (smelt roe)—These can be used interchangeably and are great for garnish and added texture.

Lemon—Lemon slices can add some nice color and go well with many different types of fish. Salmon is always a nice match.

Negi (green onion)—Slice really thin (see page 29) and use for garnish. Goes especially well with hamachi and hikarimono (shiny-skin fish) like saba (mackerel) and kohada (gizzard shad).

Furikake (rice seasoning)—This is a dry Japanese condiment that's typically mixed into rice to give it more flavor. There are many different variations, but it's usually a mix of dried fish flakes, seaweed, sesame seeds, and other dried vegetables. It's a great addition to temarizushi if you want to add variety.

Have all ingredients including toppings prepared prior to making the temari.

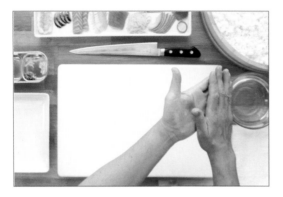

1. Wet both hands by dipping into the tezu or cold water. Make sure to spread it across both hands thoroughly. The palms should be wet and shiny but not dripping.

2. Take about 2 tablespoons (25 to 30 grams) of sushi rice and form it into a ball. Try not to squish the rice, just enough where it holds its shape.

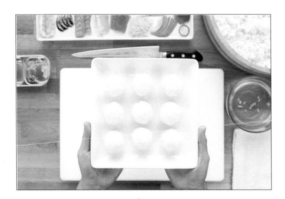

3. Transfer to a plate and cover with plastic wrap. Do this for all nine balls.

4. Take a sheet of plastic wrap and place the toppings for one ball onto the middle. Note that this is flipped, so if you're using multiple ingredients, the one you want on top will have to be placed first.

5. Place one rice ball on top of the toppings and wrap the plastic around the ball.

6. Hold the ball in one hand and tighten it by twisting the plastic. This should shape it into a nice sphere.

7. Set aside (still in the plastic) and repeat for the remaining balls.

8. When all pieces are done, unwrap each ball and place on a serving plate.

9. Garnish with toppings of choice (see page 171 for recommendations).

10. Serve with a side of wasabi, ginger, and soy sauce. Don't forget to take pictures of your work of art!

Chirashizushi (Scattered Sushi)

Chirashi sushi—also called chirashizushi or "scattered sushi"—is a style of sushi where the toppings are either placed or scattered (as the name refers) on a bed of sushi rice. There are different styles of chirashi depending on the region in Japan. For example, in the Tokyo area it is typically a bowl of sushi rice layered with an assortment of colorful cuts of sashimi and vegetables, often referred to as "chirashi-don" (don is short for donburi, which means "bowl"). Chirashi-don is probably the most popular and what we typically see at restaurants in the United States. A non-sushi rice version of this is called kaisen-don, which means "seafood bowl."

In the Kansai region of Japan (around Osaka), chirashi sushi is called "barazushi." Rather than cuts of sashimi layered on a bowl, it's usually filled with more vegetables and small cubes of cooked seafood and sometimes raw fish. But different parts of Japan have their own versions of this style of chirashi and it can be called various names. It's confusing, to say the least. For the purpose of this book and to keep things simple. I'll refer to the Tokyo style (using sashimi pieces) as "chirashi-don" and the mixed version as "barazushi."

Both are seen as festive meals and often eaten during holidays in Japan, especially on March 3rd, which is called Hinamatsuri ("girl's day" or "doll festival"). Barazushi is served in a larger bowl or a traditional sushi oke / hangiri (wooden sushi mixing bowl), which makes it perfect for parties and potlucks!

CHIRASHI-DON/KAISEN-DON (SCATTERED SUSHI BOWL/ SEAFOOD BOWL)

Simple and elegant defines this style of chirashi sushi. Fresh cuts of sashimi and colorful vegetables artistically layered on a bed of sushi rice. It may sound intimidating, but it's actually one of the easiest types of sushi to make. The most important thing is to have quality ingredients. In the recipe below, I use a variety of different seafood, but you're free to change it however you like. It is good to have at least 4 to 5 different types of sashimi, preferably more, and a couple vegetables to accompany it.

Makes: 1 bowl

Tools/Supplies:
- Cutting board
- Knife
- Clean damp towel
- Serving bowl

- Bowl for cold water or tezu (rice vinegar water; see page 12)—optional
- Moribashi (garnishing chopsticks)—optional

Ingredients:

- 1 piece amaebi (sweet shrimp) with head (see step 1)
- 1½–2 cups cooked sushi rice (unseasoned rice if making kaisen-don; see page 81)
- 1 tablespoon tsuma (shredded daikon radish; see page 26)
- 1–2 shiso leaf
- 3 slices sashimi cut maguro (tuna; see page 65)
- 3 slices sashimi cut sake (salmon; see page 65)
- 3 slices sashimi cut hamachi (yellowtail; see page 65)
- 2 slices sashimi cut tako (octopus; see page 75)
- 3–5 pieces uni (sea urchin)
- 1 tablespoon ikura (salmon roe)
- Wasabi
- Gari (pickled ginger)
- Soy sauce

Making chirashi-don or kaisen-don is not difficult; you're basically just placing the toppings onto a bed of rice. However, to make it pleasing to the eye might take a bit of practice. I'll go over some general tips and recommendations as we go through the steps, but there's really no rules, so let your creative juices flow and have fun with it!

Have all ingredients and toppings prepared.

1. For this recipe, the amaebi is peeled with the head still intact. To do this, simply peel the shell starting right under the head and work your way to the tail, but leave the tail on.

2. Using your hands or a shamoji (rice paddle), place sushi rice in the bowl and gently flatten the top.

3. Place the tsuma first. This is a garnish and should be placed in the background; it also helps stand the ingredients up.

4. Next, lay the shiso leaf on top of the tsuma. The bright color of the shiso leaf makes for great contrast but shouldn't be the focal point. Lay these under a bright-colored fish and have the top partially sticking out.

5. I lay the amaebi right in the middle since we only have one piece of it. Also the "amaebi no atama," or the head of the sweet shrimp, can be used for great decorative purposes. You cannot eat these as is, but you can deep-fry them either in a tempura batter or simply on their own.

6. The maguro goes on next, toward the back partially against the shiso and daikon. Fish with bold colors like maguro can be in the back but still stand out thanks to its rich color.

7. Salmon has a bright color as well and is placed on the other side.

8. Lighter-color fish like hamachi is better placed in front of other bold-color fish.

9. Tako doesn't have much color except for the skin, so place it in a way the skin side can be seen.

10. Smaller ingredients like uni or ikura are versatile and can be placed really anywhere. In this case the uni is rather large so I placed them all the way in front, which contrasted the colors nicely.

11. Spoon the ikura in the center, add some wasabi and ginger, and serve with a side of soy sauce.

This is just one way to plate a chirashi-don, and every chef has their own preferred method. It'll obviously depend on what type of fish and ingredients you have as well. But remember these general guidelines, and you'll be a pro in no time!

- Tsuma should be in the background and can be used to stand ingredients up.
- Shiso leaves add a lot of color and contrast and can be used as dividers between different fish. But don't overdo it; you don't want your chirashi-don to look like a salad.
- Slices of cucumber can also be used for garnish and a divider. They can also add some good texture to the bowl.
- Taller ingredients—as well as bold-colored fish—should be laid toward the back.
- You can add wasabi and ginger to the bowl or leave it on the side. Soy sauce should always be on the side.
- Remember, don't overdo it. Elegance is key.

BARAZUSHI (KANSAI-STYLE SCATTERED SUSHI)

This style might be closer to what you imagine when talking about "scattered" sushi, since you literally scatter the ingredients on a big bed of sushi rice. Each ingredient is cut smaller and usually there's more vegetables compared to the sashimi-focused chirashi-don. There are many different versions of this and there's no right or wrong. The recipe below is how I like to make ours but again, you're free to add or change any of it to your preference.

NOTE—Making the barazushi mix from scratch allows control over what ingredients go in and how much flavor you want to add in. However, if you are pressed for time, there are premade chirashi mix varieties that come in convenient little packets. All you have to do is mix it into fresh cooked rice. Look up "chirashi sushi mix" online or try to find it at any Japanese grocery market. Some well-known brands are Nagatanien, Mizkan, and Shirakiku.

Makes: 4–5 servings

Tools/Supplies:
- Cutting board
- Knife
- Medium pot or saucepan
- Medium frying pan
- Small saucepan
- Sieve
- Otoshibuta (drop lid or aluminum foil; see page 9)
- Bowl for cold water or tezu (rice vinegar water; see page 12)
- Paper towel
- Clean damp towel
- Large shallow bowl for serving (a small sushi oke/hangiri works well)
- Moribashi (garnishing chopsticks)—optional

Ingredients:

Sushi Rice
- 5 cups cooked sushi rice (see page 81 on sushi rice)

Barazushi Mix
- 4 dried shiitake mushrooms
- ¾ cup water (to soak shiitake mushrooms)

- 1 aburaage (deep-fried tofu)
- ½ carrot
- ¾ cup dashi stock (see page 201)
- 2 tablespoons sake (Japanese rice wine)
- 2 tablespoons soy sauce
- 2 tablespoons mirin (Japanese sweet rice wine)
- 1 tablespoons sugar

Kinshi Tamago (shredded egg crepe)
- 3 large eggs
- 1 teaspoon mirin (Japanese sweet rice wine)
- Pinch of salt
- 1 teaspoon corn or potato starch (optional)
- 1 tablespoon water (optional)
- Vegetable oil (or other neutral-flavored oil)

Toppings
- 6–8 snow or snap peas
- 5–6 ounces broiled unagi (freshwater eel; about ½ fillet; see pages 63 and 70)
- 8 ounces sashimi grade salmon (cut into cubes)
- 4–5 tablespoons ikura (salmon roe)
- 2 tablespoons kizami nori (shredded dried seaweed)

MAKE SUSHI RICE

1. Follow instructions on making sushi rice (see page 81). To save time, you can start preparing the barazushi mix while you wait for the rice to cook.

PREPARE BARAZUSHI MIX

1. Gather all ingredients.

2. Add the water and dried shiitake mushrooms in a bowl and let soak for 15 to 20 minutes. To fully submerge the shiitake, place a small cup or bowl on top.

3. While the shiitake soaks, cut the aburaage in half lengthwise and slice ¼-inch strips.

4. Peel the carrot, cut it into ⅛-inch-thick slices, and then lay them down neatly.

5. Now julienne cut them into roughly ⅛-inch-thick sticks.

6. After soaking the shiitake, squeeze out excess liquid from each and be sure to save the liquid. This is shiitake dashi stock that we'll be using to cook our ingredients.

7. Strain the stock using a fine sieve into the pot or saucepan.

8. Cut off the stems from the shiitake and slice very thin.

9. Add the dashi stock in the pot with the shiitake stock.

10. Add the sliced shiitake mushrooms and aburaage to the pot. Turn the heat to medium-high and wait for it to start boiling. Once it boils, use a ladle or fine sieve to skim the foam off the surface.

11. Now add the carrots, sake, soy sauce, mirin, and sugar and stir gently.

12. Lower the heat to a simmer (about medium-low) and cover with an otoshibuta (drop lid); simmer for 12 to 15 minutes. Make sure to occasionally take a peek to check the liquid level; turn down the heat if it's evaporating too fast.

13. Most of the liquid should now be reduced. Take off heat and let cool (with the otoshibuta still on). If you want to cool it down faster, you can transfer it onto a large plate and spread it out. The chirashizushi mix is now finished!

MAKE KINSHI TAMAGO (SHREDDED EGG CREPE)

Used as garnish in a lot of Japanese cuisine, kinshi tamago is basically thin strips of an egg crepe (called usuyaki tamago) and adds a vibrant color, texture, and some extra protein.

1. Add eggs, mirin, and salt to a bowl and beat the eggs. Try not to whisk too much air into the mixture.

2. Optional step. Strain the egg mixture into a container preferably with a spout. This step will help even out the color.

3. Mix cornstarch and water in a separate bowl until it's an even slurry. Add it to the egg and mix together. This step helps keep the egg more intact but is also optional.

4. Heat the frying pan over medium heat. Fold or ball up a paper towel and using chopsticks, dip it into some vegetable oil and apply to the pan. Make sure to coat the entire surface evenly.

5. Lower the heat and pour enough egg mixture to evenly coat the bottom. Do this by tilting and swirling the pan so that the egg makes a nice circle. Depending on the size of your pan, you might want to separate into two or three batches.

6. Cook until the edges start to dry and can be easily peeled from the pan (about 30 to 40 seconds usually) and then flip using a spatula.

7. Let it cook for about 10 to 15 more seconds and transfer to a plate. Repeat steps until the egg mixture is gone. Set aside to cool.

8. Once the crepe is completely cooled, take a sheet and roll it up gently.

9. Cut into thin strips and loosen it up. Repeat with the other crepes and set aside.

SNOW PEAS OR SNAP PEAS

1. First, remove the firm stringy fiber from the edges.

2. Boil water in a small saucepan and add a pinch of salt. Once water boils, blanch the snow peas for 1½ minutes. Have an ice bath ready.

3. Transfer to a bowl of ice water immediately. This will stop it from overcooking.

4. Once cooled, pat dry using a paper towel and cut each piece diagonally in half. If the peas are really large, you might have to cut into thirds.

5. Repeat for the remaining peas and set aside.

UNAGI (FRESHWATER EEL)

1. Slice the broiled unagi lengthwise down the middle in half (see page 63 on how to broil).

2. Next, cut crosswise into roughly ½-inch squares and set aside.

SALMON

1. Cut salmon into ½-inch-wide strips either lengthwise or crosswise.

2. Take the wider strips and cut them in half if needed.

3. Now take each strip and cut them into roughly ½-inch cubes. Transfer to a bowl, cover with plastic, and leave in the refrigerator until ready to use.

PUTTING EVERYTHING TOGETHER

Congratulations on finishing the prep! Now it's time to combine all your hard work into the finished product.

1. Gently squeeze out any excess liquid from the chirashizushi mix. Add mix to the sushi rice and discard liquid.

2. Use a large bowl or a sushi oke and mix evenly throughout the rice.

3. Transfer to a large shallow bowl (or keep it in the sushi oke if serving in it) and lay the kinshi tamago evenly across the rice.

4. Assemble the remaining toppings. Scatter the salmon and unagi, then place the snow peas so that the pointy ends faceup. I usually like to put either two or three in bunches. And then dollop the ikura using a spoon.

3. Strain the liquid through a sieve and into a pot or saucepan. This is the shiitake broth that we'll be cooking in.

4. Add shiitake mushrooms, sugar, soy sauce, and mirin to the pot and lightly stir.

5. Bring to a boil and then turn down heat to low. Simmer for 20 to 25 minutes. Transfer the shiitake and let cool on a plate.

6. Once cool to touch, cut shiitake into thin slices.

7. Using your hands, lightly squeeze excess moisture out.

8. Finished!

> **NOTE**—Make sure to check on the liquid level occasionally. If the liquid is reducing too fast, the heat is probably too high. Turn it down and add a little water so the shiitake doesn't burn.

MISO-SHIRU (MISO SOUP)

Miso soup ("miso-shiru" or "omiso-shiru") is a staple not only in Japanese restaurants but in every Japanese household. Every family has their own recipe, and ingredients can widely vary. But the one I personally find most comforting (even to this day) is the simplest version my mom made when I was a child. The ingredients include dashi, miso, tofu, wakame (type of seaweed), and a little bit of negi (green onion), and that's it. Not only are the ingredients simple, but the process is even easier. Below is the recipe, which you're free to alter to your own preference and/or add other ingredients.

Makes: 4 servings

Tools/Supplies:
- Medium pot or saucepan
- Sieve (optional)
- Whisk (optional)
- Knife
- Ladle

Ingredients:
- 4 cups dashi stock (see page 201)
- 4 tablespoons awase miso (combination of red and white miso)
- 7 ounces soft or silken tofu cut into ½-inch cubes
- 2 tablespoons dried wakame
- 1 negi (green onion)—thinly sliced (see page 29)

Instructions:

1. Add the dashi stock to the pot and bring to a simmer.
2. Add in the miso. Put the miso in a sieve and place it in the dashi. Gently press the miso through with a spoon to make it dissolve faster. You can also whisk in the miso as well.
3. After the miso has completely dissolved, add the tofu cubes and dried wakame.
4. Bring soup to a light simmer and turn off the heat; do not boil. Boiling miso soup will alter its flavor.
5. Garnish with negi right before serving.

SHRIMP TEMPURA

Tempura is one of the most popular and well-known dishes that's served all around the world. It's lightly battered seafood or vegetables that's deep-fried until it has a golden, crispy shell. You can eat it by itself, with noodles (soba and udon are common), on top of rice such as a tempura donburi or tendon (tempura rice bowl), and of course inside a sushi roll. Typically, shrimp is used for tempura sushi, but you can easily swap vegetables such as asparagus, zucchini, and carrots. Experiment to find out what you like!

Makes: 6 pieces

Tools/Supplies
- Large pot or wok (a deep skillet or deep fryer works as well)
- Chopsticks or tongs
- Sifter
- Wire rack with baking pan underneath (a paper towel–lined plate works as well)
- Large bowl
- Sieve or spider strainer
- Deep fry thermometer (optional)

Ingredients
- 6 shrimps or prawns—(black tiger shrimp or Japanese tiger prawn is best, but any other large shrimp works as well.) If you want to save time get tail on, deveined, pre-peeled shrimp.
- Neutral-flavored oil (vegetable, canola, corn, etc.). Enough to fill your pot/wok a little above halfway.
- Sesame oil (add to frying oil; use 10:1 ratio of neutral-flavored oil to sesame oil)
- All-purpose flour

Tempura Batter
- 1 large egg
- 1½ cups ice cold water
- 1 cup all-purpose flour or tempurako (tempura flour; see page 16)

PREPARING THE SHRIMP

1. Peel the shrimp, but make sure to keep the tail intact.

2. Devein the shrimp by cutting a line down the middle of the back and cleaning out the entrails. Rinse the shrimp gently in cold water and dry using paper towels.

3. Remove the dirt and moisture out of the tail by carefully using the tip of your knife to scrape it out. This will prevent the tails from exploding in the oil, so do not skip this step!

4. Cut small slits along the underbelly of the shrimp at a diagonal, roughly 5 to 6 times depending on the size of your shrimp.

5. Flip the shrimp over so that the back is facing up. Gently push down on the shrimp from one end to the other so that it straightens out. You should hear almost a "cracking" sound every time you push down.

6. The shrimp should be straight and about 1 to 2 inches longer than it originally was. Repeat for the remaining shrimp.

FRYING THE SHRIMP

1. Fill a large pot/wok/deep skillet with at least 2 inches of oil and start to heat on medium (to 350°F). While the oil heats up, gather all ingredients for tempura batter.

2. Crack the egg into a large bowl and start breaking it up. Add the cold water and whisk till it's fully combined.

3. Sift the flour into the mixture and mix the batter (chopsticks work best here). Make sure to not overmix; it's better to leave small clumps. Leave in refrigerator if not using right away.

4. Check oil temperature—340 to 350°F (170 to 180°C).

5. Lightly coat each shrimp with all-purpose flour and set aside.

6. Hold the shrimp by the tail and coat it by dunking it into the batter. Lift it up and let the excess batter drip off. Now carefully place it into the oil while holding onto the tail still. If your oil is deep enough, gently swing the shrimp back and forth in a slow rocking motion. Do this for about 3 seconds and let go. This helps the shrimp to stay straight, which will be easier to roll in sushi.

7. Deep-fry the shrimp until golden-brown (usually around 2 minutes but depends on the size). You don't want to overcrowd the oil; try to use about half of the space at a time. Transfer shrimp onto a wire rack or paper towel–lined plate. If you are making more than one batch, use the sieve or spider strainer to clean out the extra flakes that are left in the oil in between batches.

8. Continue frying the rest of the shrimp.

PRO TIP—Maintaining oil temperature is the most important thing when it comes to tempura. Using a deep fry thermometer is the most accurate, or you can be old-school and do a batter check. Dip your chopsticks into the batter and drip some into the oil. If it starts to sink and barely touches the bottom and comes right back up, you're ready to go. If it stays on the bottom, it's too cold and if it doesn't sink at all then it's too hot. Adjust temperature accordingly.

If you're planning on eating tempura on its own there's a method called "hana-age" that will level up your tempura game (just like at a Japanese tempura restaurant). Hana-age translates to "flower-fry" and is a traditional method that's used to give tempura more volume and a crispier outer layer. When the batter hits the hot oil, it sort of looks like a flower blooming, hence the name.

Congratulations, you now know how to make shrimp tempura! You can use this same technique to fry vegetables and other proteins as well. Experiment and see what you like!

TEMPURA "HANA-AGE"

There are different methods on how to do this, but the simplest and the original way my dad taught me is to use chopsticks. After you place your shrimp (or any other ingredient) into the hot oil, using your chopsticks, lightly drizzle some batter right on top of it. When you do this, shake the chopsticks so that the falling batter are small bits versus a stream. Immediately tap on the shrimp with your chopsticks so that the batter breaks apart into smaller flakes. Don't tap on it too hard though where the batter flies off. Keep repeating this process so that you cover the entire shrimp. It's also a good technique to lightly hit your chopstick on the edge of the pot/wok to shake off any excess batter onto the shrimp. This will help give it even more crispiness and volume.

TAMAGOYAKI

Tamagoyaki is the general Japanese term for a rolled omelet and is a staple in Japanese cuisine. There is also "dashimaki tamago" and "atsuyaki tamago," which are versions of tamagoyaki. Dashimaki is basically a rolled omelet with dashi in it, while atsuyaki just means "thick-cooked," which is typically the style that sushi restaurants make. Tamagoyaki for sushi is usually sweetened, almost cake-like at times, and often labeled "egg custard." The sweet but savory flavor is a great way to finish off the meal, so it's often served last. It's also a way for sushi chefs to showcase their skill. Because tamagoyaki takes skill to make well, the quality of the tamago represents the quality of the restaurant.

Personally, I favor more of a savory tamagoyaki, so the recipe I share with you is more toward the savory vs sweet side. We'll cook it "thick" so it's an atsuyaki, but since it also has dashi in it, it'll be a dashimaki tamago. I figure I would show you the best of both worlds. Tamagoyaki is something that takes a lot of practice and patience (and a lot of eggs). So even if it doesn't go right the first time (or the tenth), keep trying! This doesn't have to go with sushi; it's a great bento item or a treat eaten by itself. It can be great for kiddos, and it's one of our son's favorites!

Makes: 10–12 pieces

Tools/Supplies
- Tamagoyaki frying pan or medium/large frying pan
- Chopsticks
- 2 large bowls
- Small bowl
- Whisk
- Strainer
- Ladle
- Spatula
- Small bowl for oil
- Paper towel
- Makisu (bamboo rolling mat)—optional

Ingredients
- 1 teaspoon soy sauce
- 1½ tablespoon mirin (Japanese sweet rice wine)
- 1 tablespoon sugar
- ¼ teaspoon salt
- 8 large eggs
- ⅔ cup dashi stock (see page 201)
- Vegetable oil

TAMAGOYAKI MIXTURE

1. Gather all ingredients.

2. In a small bowl, add soy sauce, mirin, sugar, and salt and stir well.

3. Crack open eggs in a large bowl and gently stir using a whisk. Pour in the soy sauce mixture.

4. Whisk the egg mixture using a side-to-side motion, always touching the bottom of the bowl with the whisk. This prevents too much air from getting into the mixture.

5. Add the dashi stock and mix using the same side-to-side motion.

6. Strain the egg mixture into another bowl. This will catch any possible shells and smooth out the mixture.

COOKING TAMAGOYAKI

1. Place the pan over medium heat. While you wait for it to heat up, prepare a small bowl of vegetable oil and a balled-up paper towel. Let the paper towel sit in the oil.

2. Oil the pan thoroughly with the paper towel. Make sure to get the edges and corners.

3. Drop a small bit of the egg onto the pan to test the heat. The egg should start to turn white and slightly sizzle.

4. Ladle in the egg mixture and quickly tilt the pan so that you have a thin layer covering the entire surface. Depending on the size of your pan and ladle you may need to add more. Poke any air bubbles using chopsticks.

5. While the egg on the top surface is still soft, start rolling the sheet from the far side, making your way to the handle side. When you do this, focus on using the hand that's holding the pan to "flip" the egg with momentum. The chopsticks are used to guide the egg in the right direction.

6. When the egg is rolled all the way to the handle side, apply oil to the opposite side using the oiled paper towel.

7. Slide the egg to the far end and apply oil now to the handle side. Sometimes it helps to tap the pan a bit to unstick the egg from the edges.

8. With the egg now on the far end, pour in another ladle of the egg mixture. Tilt the pan toward the far end slightly and lift the rolled egg with your chopsticks to allow the new egg mixture to run underneath. Do this evenly across.

 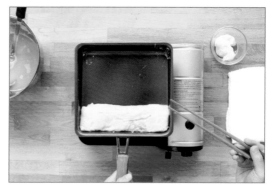

9. Wait till the new egg mixture has solidified a bit (but with the top still soft) and then start rolling the egg from the far side down to the handle side.

10. Shake the pan slightly to help the egg detach from the side of the pan. While using the chopsticks as a guide, focus on the hand that's holding the pan to flip the egg with momentum. Fold over twice and you should be at the bottom of the pan. You can also use a spatula to help flip it.

11. Repeat steps 6 through 10 until the mixture runs out.

12. On the last round, use a spatula and gently push the tamagoyaki against the walls of the pan (if using a square tamagoyaki pan). This will help shape it into a cleaner rectangle.

13. When finished cooking but while it's still hot, wrap the tamagoyaki in a makisu. Place the overlap of the makisu on the bottom or you can wrap a couple rubber bands around it to help keep its shape. Let cool for 5 to 10 minutes.

14. Remove from the makisu. Plate, and serve with a side of soy sauce and some grated daikon radish.

NOTE—Tamagoyaki is great on its own or of course you can use it for sushi. For nigirizushi, cut it crosswise into about ⅜-inch-thick slices. For chirashi-don, cut it about ½ inch thick and then cut that diagonally into two pieces. If serving by itself, add a side of grated daikon and some soy sauce.

HOMEMADE PICKLED GINGER (GARI)

Making gari at home is simple, and it's even easier when you follow my sushi vinegar recipe (see page 86). That same sushi vinegar that you use to make sushi rice can be used to pickle your own ginger. In my opinion, it'll taste much better than store-bought ones, not to mention there's no added preservatives. So next time you're preparing sushi rice, make extra sushi vinegar and use it for a homemade jar of gari. It's the little details that'll impress all your sushi-loving friends!

Makes: 1½ cups

Tools/Supplies:
- Medium bowl
- Medium pot or saucepan
- Strainer
- Tray
- Paper towel
- Airtight container or glass jar

Ingredients:
- 8 ounces young ginger root (peeled and washed)
- ½ tablespoon kosher salt
- 1½ cup sushi vinegar (see page 86)

Instructions:

1. Peel and wash ginger roots.
2. Slice very thin using a knife, peeler, or mandolin. You can also julienne cut them into small strips instead. Place them into a bowl.
3. Add the salt onto the sliced ginger and gently massage it in. Set aside for 10 minutes.
4. While waiting for the ginger, bring a pot of water to a boil. When it boils, blanch the ginger for 1 minute and then drain using a strainer or sieve.
5. Once cooled to touch, place the ginger slices on a paper towel–lined tray and pat dry.
6. Add the ginger slices into a glass jar or airtight container.
7. Make the sushi vinegar and pour it into the jar while it's still hot. The sushi vinegar recipe doesn't require extreme heat, but if it was heated up too high, wait until it cools down a bit or transfer the sliced ginger into a more heat-safe container such as a stainless bowl and then pour the hot sushi vinegar in. Then transfer it back to the jar when it cools.
8. Mix the ginger and make sure it's submerged in the sushi vinegar.
9. Allow it to cool to room temperature and then move to refrigerator. Let it soak for a minimum of 24 hours (3 days+ is ideal). Gari can last up to 6 months in the refrigerator if stored in an airtight container.

Presentation

With Japanese cuisine, the presentation or "moritsuke" is an extremely important factor and chefs often dedicate a tremendous effort into making the dish beautiful, like a work of art. There's a saying in Japanese, "me de taberu," which literally translates to "eat with eyes." The belief is, to fully appreciate and experience the meal, we "eat" or enjoy the beauty of the dish with our eyes first and then with our palates afterward. Sushi is obviously one of those cuisines where presentation plays a big role, and a lot of times it's the small things that can make a big difference. Whether you are making sushi for the first time or are trying to hone your skills, you worked hard to make your beautiful dish. So, let's make it show well! In the following pages, you'll find some basic tips on how to present your sushi and some simple garnishes that can level up your sushi game.

SUSHI ROLLS

Pretty sushi requires pretty rolling, and that starts all the way back from making the sushi rice. It's a domino effect; if the ingredients are messy then the final product will be messy as well. Another important step is the cutting. No matter how perfect the roll may be, if it's not cut well, then it'll look sloppy. But how you plate plays a big role as well. So here are some very basic and simple techniques that you can use when plating your rolls.

- **Place each piece at an angle (uramaki)**—This is probably the most common way rolls are presented at restaurants. It's simple, elegant, and super easy to do. Once the roll is cut, place it straight onto the plate and then turn each piece at about a 30- to 45-degree angle (either direction is fine). The more you rotate each piece, the longer the roll will look. Focus on where each piece touches each other throughout the roll (it should be the same across); this will help keep the placement nice and straight.

- **Lay some pieces down**—A combination of pieces that are upright next to some that are laid down can have a nice contrast and show the inside ingredients better. Especially if you have an end piece with the ingredient sticking out, for example shrimp tempura roll or spider roll.

- **Same height (hosomaki)**—This is especially the case for any hosomaki, and it goes back to the importance of cutting. Hosomaki is typically placed upright, but when the pieces are uneven, it can look very sloppy. Though sometimes it's done on purpose to make it look like steps or cut at an angle for design. If your pieces come out uneven, try moving them around to get the closest match next to each other. You can also place these at an angle (by twos).

- **Sauce Sauce Sauce**—If the roll you're making goes well with sauce such as unagi sauce or spicy mayo, use it to your advantage. Don't drown the thing, but you can drizzle it on top to "hide" minor defects or make a design with it as well. Pay attention to what type of plate you use if you plan to use sauce.

- **Negative space**—Don't be afraid to leave some space on the plate. It's easy to want to pack the plate or platter with a bunch of sushi, but less can be more. Simple and elegant is always a good way to go.

- **Creative plates**—Play with different types of plating. It doesn't even have to be a plate. That wood cutting board that you got as a white elephant gift last year may be perfect! One of my favorite photos that I took a while back was an assortment of nigirizushi on a candle holder. Look around your house and see what you can use. The most important thing is to experiment and have fun! Making it pretty is always nice, but don't stress over it (unless you're a professional sushi chef, then perhaps you need to). There's nothing wrong with eating it right off the cutting board either; best to eat it fresh!

NIGIRIZUSHI

Plating nigirizushi is typically simpler than plating rolls. I usually like to tilt each piece at an angle with the same fish grouped together. But it all depends on how many pieces, what type of fish, and what plate you're using. Simple garnishes and toppings can be a great addition as well. They add flavor, texture, and color, which can be the difference between a good piece and great piece.

SASHIMI

I go over presentation tips for sashimi in the sashimi section (see page 77), so be sure to check that out.

GARNISHES

Garnishing can add interest, dimension, and make a plate look complete. You don't have to have expert knife skills for a lot of them. The ones I'm sharing with you are very simple and can go well on any sushi plate.

Cucumber Slices

The easiest and very versatile garnish. You can use these to separate different fish or just leave them on the side to add some color.

1. Cut a small section of the cucumber crosswise.

2. Now cut that piece lengthwise in half.

3. Place the flat side down and cut slices crosswise about ⅛ inch thick. You can cut however many pieces, but usually 5 or so makes for a nice garnish.

4. Fan out the slices horizontally and stand them up or like a fan to make it look like leaves. You can also cut them at an angle to make longer slices.

Lemon Bowl

These are great for smaller toppings such as ikura, tobiko, or any type of roe/caviar.

1. Slice the lemon in half crosswise.

2. Then, cut off the end crosswise (roughly about ⅓).

3. Using the tip of your knife, insert it right where the inner part meets the skin. Following the skin line, cut out the inner part by rotating the lemon.

4. Place the end piece at the bottom of the lemon skin to make a small lemon bowl.

Citrus Twists

Extremely simple and elegant garnish you can add to a plate. You can use lemons, limes, key limes, or small oranges.

1. Slice citrus crosswise at about an ⅛ inch thick.

2. Make a straight cut halfway to the center of each slice.

3. Twist the citrus slices by spreading the cut ends to opposite sides.

4. Lay multiple slices together to make a spiral design.

Wasabi Leaf

This works if you're using imitation wasabi; real wasabi will not form like this. You can shape and design them into anything you like; get creative!

1. Take a ball of wasabi and shape it into a leaf.

2. Using a toothpick or something thin, press on the wasabi to make a leaf design—one line down the center and then smaller lines from the center line to the edge of the leaf.

Sake and Other Drink Pairings

This might be my favorite part of the entire book! Whether you're into beer, wine, sake, or nonalcoholic beverages, there's always something that will pair nicely with sushi. Full disclosure, I'm not a sommelier or sake-brewing specialist, but I do enjoy a well-crafted, well-thought-out drink pairing, especially with sushi and Japanese cuisine. I share with you my knowledge and personal experiences through the guide, tips, and recommendations below. What I find enjoyable may not necessarily suit your personal preference, and that is okay. Ultimately, what you drink (or not drink) is up to you. But I hope that I can expand your drink-pairing horizon to make your next sushi meal that much more delightful. Kanpai!

SAKE (NIHON-SHU)

We all know sake as the rice "wine" that comes hot or cold and is served at practically any Japanese restaurant. But the word "sake" actually refers to the general term "alcohol" in

Sake barrels at Meiji-Jingu Shrine, Tokyo, Japan (credit; © dreamstime.com / Hai Huy Ton That)

ULTIMATE SAKE GUIDE

SAKE GRADE LEVELS

NON-JUMMAI
Brewed using Rice, Water, Yeast, Koji Mold, and Distilled Brewers Alcohol.

DAIGINJO

GINJO

HONJOZO

FUTSU-SHU (Table Sake)
Usually mass produced with automated brewing processes and high amounts of distilled alcohol.

JUNMAI
"Pure Rice" - Brewed using ONLY Rice, Water, Yeast, and Koji Mold.

JUNMAI DAIGINJO

JUNMAI GINJO

JUNMAI

RICE MILLING
Rice polished down to:

AT LEAST **50%**
(50% or more milled away)

AT LEAST **60%**
(40% or more milled away)

AT LEAST **70%**
(30% or more milled away)

FUTSU-SHU (Table Sake)
No Minimum Requirements
Usually anywhere between 70-93%

(Left vertical scale: SUPER PREMIUM / PREMIUM / LOW GRADE)

SAKE TEMPERATURE CHART

JAPANESE NAME	ENGLISH TRANSLATION	TEMPERATURE
TOBIKIRIKAN	VERY HOT SAKE	133°F / 55°C
ATSUKAN	HOT SAKE	122°F / 50°C
JOKAN	SLIGHTLY HOT SAKE	113°F / 45°C
NARUKAN	WARM SAKE	104°F / 40°C
HITOHADAKAN	BODY TEMPERATURE	95°F / 35°C
HINATAKAN	SUNBATHING	86°F / 30°C
JO-ON	ROOM TEMPERATURE	68°F / 20°C
SUZUHIE	AUTUMN BREEZE	59°F / 15°C
HANAHIE	CHILLED SPRING FLOWER	51°F / 10°C
YUKIHIE	WINTER SNOW	41°F / 5°C
MIZORE-ZAKE	SAKE SLUSHIE	23°F / -5°C

GENERAL TEMPERATURE EFFECT

WARMING
- Fuller body
- Richer flavors
- Brings out umami
- Enhances savory flavors
- Reduces bitterness
- Overheating will increase alcohol intensity and dryness

CHILLING
- Crisper body
- Cleaner flavors
- Enhanced Ginjo flavors and aroma (light, fruity, fragrant, etc)
- Over-chilling can result to bitterness and loss of delicate flavors and aromas

SMV (SAKE METER VALUE) CHART

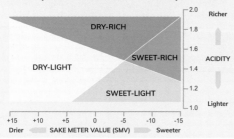

DRY-RICH

SWEET-RICH

DRY-LIGHT

SWEET-LIGHT

Richer — 2.0 / 1.8 / 1.6 / 1.4 / 1.2 / 1.0 — Lighter

ACIDITY

+15 +10 +5 0 -5 -10 -15
Drier — SAKE METER VALUE (SMV) — Sweeter

GENERAL FLAVOR PROFILE & PAIRINGS

	Flavor Profile	Pairing Recommendations	Temperature
Daiginjo / Junmai Daiginjo	Exquisite floral aroma, rich, lush and refined fruit flavors, subtle umami finish	Shellfish, sushi and sashimi (especially white fish), uni, brie cheese, light Asian cuisine. Avoid rich umami such as heavy soy sauce or miso. Also avoid really oily or meaty dishes.	Chilled
Ginjo / Junmai Ginjo	Light, dry, fruity, softer body, floral aroma	Simple light dishes (edamame, caprese, carpaccio), sushi and sashimi, Chinese style steamed fish and other mild fish dishes. Avoid really rich flavored dishes.	Chilled, Room Temp
Junmai	Rich, full body, umami-forward, earthiness, slightly acidic flavor	Heavy seasoned rice dishes (fried rice), red meats, fatty meats (pork belly), yakitori, fried chicken, katsu, teriyaki, high umami flavored vegetables (mushrooms, asparagus, artichokes).	Chilled, Room Temp, Warm
Honjozo	Light, dry, pleasantly acidic, earthy	Wide range of dishes, light or heavy. Sushi, hot pot, tempura, wagyu, grilled meats, steaks, fish and chips, spicy Asian food.	Chilled, Room Temp, Warm

Japanese. The correct word usage is "Nihon-shu," which translates to "Japanese alcohol" and that's what we'll dive into a little deeper here now. But for the purpose of this book, I will use the general term "sake" to refer to rice wine.

Sake has become a staple at any sushi restaurant (at least in the United States), but little do people know that traditionally, sake is not paired with sushi. The reason for that is because sake is made from rice (hence "rice wine"), and it's thought that eating sushi and drinking sake together will fill you up too fast. Now that doesn't mean sushi restaurants in Japan won't carry any sake, especially in modern days, but they may recommend something else (such as wine or beer) to go with the sushi you ordered. Sashimi, on the other hand, is a completely different story. Since sashimi has no rice, sake is seen to be the perfect pairing to go along with it.

That said, there's nothing wrong with pairing your favorite sushi with sake. Personally, I get a lot fuller drinking beer. Where it matters is what type of sake you choose to drink. There are many different styles of sake and thousands of different labels, and each has its own flavor profile. You don't want the sake to overpower the sushi and vice versa.

I can go into this much further (probably write another book on the topic by itself), but instead I have created a cheat sheet that can be your ultimate guide to sake, and how to pair it with your favorite food (not just sushi).

BEER

When I go out to a sushi restaurant, the first drink I order is usually a cold glass of "nama" (draft beer). A perfect pour of Japanese beer (bonus if it's in a frosted glass) quenches the thirst like no other. The type of Japanese beer available in the United States is limited, but I would say Asahi (Super Dry) is one of my favorites. It's light, refreshing, and so versatile with any type of Japanese food, making it perfect to order at sushi restaurants. However, my ultimate favorite Japanese beer must be Premium Yebisu (from Sapporo brewing). Unfortunately, it's not available in the States, but I highly recommend it if you happen to come by this. It's crisp with just enough richness. Think if a German lager and Japanese pilsner had a baby together.

As for the type of beer that goes well with sushi, you really can't go wrong with any Japanese beer. If you want to venture out to other types, go for something light and crisp that won't overpower the flavors of sushi. Pilsners, Kolsch, and some pale ales go well.

WINE

Wine is a great choice for sushi, and since there's so many different varieties, there's plenty to choose from. Some say seafood can only go with white wine, but that is a myth. Yes, overall, there's more white wine that pairs well with sushi but that doesn't mean a red wine won't, and just because it's a white wine, doesn't mean it'll match with sushi. It all depends on what type of sushi you're eating and what you enjoy drinking. Below are some of my recommendations but ultimately it's up to you to see what you enjoy. So, get the bottle opener ready!

Riesling

Dry rieslings can go well with a variety of different sushi, making it a nice bottle for the

Variety of Japanese beer and sake (credit: © dreamstime.com / Artitwpd)

entire meal. If you like spicy items, a semidry riesling will serve nicely, cutting the spice and balancing out the palate with its slight sweetness. Stay away from very sweet wines.

Pinot Grigio

Pinot grigio or pinot gris is one of my go-to white wines for any seafood. A light-bodied version is good with sushi, especially with leaner fish like tai (sea bream) and hirame (flounder).

Sauvignon Blanc

New Zealand sauvignon blanc (to be specific) can go especially well with a variety of different sushi. It's light-bodied and slightly fruity with hints of citrus. The high acidity helps reset the palate as well, making a great bottle for the entire meal.

Vinho Verde

Some good friends of ours introduced this to us and we've been hooked since! We always have a bottle (or two) in our fridge. Unlike most bottles, vinho verde means "young wine" in Portuguese and doesn't specify the type of grape, which means you can have red, white, or rosé. For sushi though, I recommend the white. It's light enough to pair with a variety of fish while the slight carbonation helps cut the flavor of heavier items such as tempura.

Rosé

Rosés are great options as well, especially ones from Provence, France. Provence borders the Mediterranean Sea, so you know it's going to pair nicely with seafood, and sushi is definitely one of those cuisines.

Pinot Noir

Who said red wine can't be paired with sushi? pinot noirs are one of my favorite type of wines, so of course I would try it with sushi, and yes, it can work really well! Stick to a light-bodied one (ones from Burgundy or Willamette Valley are great options) and pair it with fatty fish such as toro, salmon, or hamachi belly.

Champagne

The classic celebration bottle. Might not be the first thing you think when pairing wine with sushi, but it actually goes really well. Think caviar . . . so ikura, tobiko, masago, and uni can be a great pairing as well. Blanc de blanc, which is a champagne that's made exclusively from white grapes (typically chardonnay), is amazing with a lot of different sashimi and of course the different roe that I mentioned. Try it out if you feel like celebrating, and why not? You put in all this time and effort to make an amazing sushi meal so go ahead, pop open that bottle and celebrate your hard work! Kanpai!

COCKTAILS/SPIRITS

If you are thinking how can piña coladas, daquiris, and anything with a tiny umbrella pair well with sushi, erase those thoughts immediately. Those are not the cocktails I am referring to. There are so many cocktails that can pair well with sushi, it just depends on what your "cocktail" is. For me, my go-to is a nice refreshing gin and tonic with hints of citrus and cucumber. Alternatively, I can't leave out my favorite gin martini—Botanist gin with dry vermouth, hint of bitters, shaken up ice cold, topped with a lemon twist . . . damn, I'll be right back. What I'm trying to say is, don't leave out the cocktails as a good pairing with sushi, especially if you're at a restaurant that has obviously put some effort into their cocktail list. Here are some that I find go well with sushi.

Gin

I must put this first because it's one of my favorite spirits! A solid gin and tonic (G&T) can go well with so many different cuisines, especially seafood. For sushi, I recommend using Hendrick's gin because of its cucumber-forward flavor. It's great with tuna, salmon, hamachi, and different whitefish as well.

Japanese Cocktails

Anything using Japanese ingredients like yuzu, ginger, or shiso is usually a safe bet to match well with sushi. The same goes with sake cocktails. Sake martini or "saketini" is a great option and you can use either vodka or gin according to your preference.

Umami-Rich Cocktails

There's two different ways you can go about pairing cocktails with sushi. First is to contrast the flavor by going with something that "cuts" the sushi (think ginger as a palate cleanser). The second is to go with something that complements it while having a similar umami flavor.

Now let's think dirty for a second: three blue cheese–stuffed olives on a metal pick, sitting in a frosted martini glass with your favorite gin (or vodka). Wait, what were you thinking about? Yes, dirty martinis can go well with sushi, so if you're a fan of martinis, give it a shot (pun intended). I also recommend margaritas with a salted rim and anything with clamato in it, such as a bloody Caesar (bloody mary using clamato).

Mezcal/Tequila

Mezcal has become one of my favorite spirits throughout the recent years. Smoky but refreshing at the same time, yes please. Tequila, though not as smoky, has a similar flavor profile, which I find goes well with many seafood dishes (think ceviche). It goes especially well with shrimp and other shellfish. Stay away from wasabi or ginger though, since the flavors tend to clash.

Whisky

Yes! I'm actually having a glass as I write this now. Whisky (or whiskey) might not seem like a good pairing with sushi, but it all depends on how and what you have it with. Japanese highball is a very well-rounded whisky cocktail that goes well with a variety of different sushi. It's light, refreshing, and versatile. *But* as a guy who likes scotch neat, it's a bit watery for my taste. So how do you pair something like a single malt scotch? Well, honestly there's not much that pairs exceptionally well. Except for dishes that have a similar smokiness to it, so think unagi. If I had to choose an all-around whisky to go with sushi, it'd be Japanese whisky. Hibiki, Nikka, other Suntory labels are all good choices. Adding ice or a bit of water can change a glass of whisky tremendously, so experiment with different styles and see what you like. If it doesn't match, then at least you have a nice glass of whisky to close out the dinner. Never can go wrong with that.

Sushi Etiquette

In the more than twenty years I've been an "itamae" or sushi chef, I've practically seen it all. From people incorrectly using chopsticks to taking sips of soy sauce. These folks are not to blame, as the etiquette of eating sushi is confusing to many. Ultimately what's important is to enjoy the meal and have a good time, while of course being polite and having general table manners. But for those interested in tradition and want to experience a more authentic sushi meal, read on. Below I share some tips and suggestions as well as answer some commonly asked questions about how to eat sushi. However, take it as a general guideline; none of these are absolute rules, and the sushi police will not be coming after you if you decide not to follow them. Think about your setting as well—your experience at a Michelin star sushi restaurant in Tokyo is going to be much different than an all-you-can-eat sushi buffet in Vegas. Both can be great in their own way, just different, and some of these "rules" may not apply depending on where you're dining. Just remember, wherever you are, the most important thing is to be kind, respectful, and enjoy what you're eating!

- **Make a reservation**—It's always good to make a reservation or at least call ahead even if the restaurant doesn't take reservations. It's especially important at smaller (a lot of times, high-end) sushi restaurants. Most traditional sushi restaurants for example in Japan are very limited in seating and will only seat you if you have a reservation (sometimes booked out for months). Make sure to let them know of any dietary restrictions since the chef will take that into account. Be on time! If you find out you are not able to fulfill your reservation, call to cancel not only as a courtesy, but some restaurants will charge you for a no-show.

- **Perfume and cologne**—Our sense of smell plays a very important role in eating (think about the last time you had a stuffy nose and tried tasting). Though it may sound obscure for some, strong perfume or cologne can ruin a meal, especially something as exquisite as sushi. Especially at tiny sushi bars, which many high-end sushi bars are in Japan.

- **Irasshaimase!**—You might've heard this (maybe even startled by it) when you enter a Japanese restaurant. Simply translated, it means "welcome" or "please come in" and is a standard greeting for Japanese establishments. There's no need to really reply, just appreciate that you're welcomed in and continue to the host or hostess.

- **Sushi bar**—Sit at the sushi bar if you want the best sushi experience. However, if your goal is to catch up with friends, then go with a table. Now that doesn't mean you can't sit at the bar if you want to chat with friends; just don't be too caught up in your own conversations where you're oblivious to what's being served. Good sushi chefs will explain what is being served as well as time it to your personal pace. It's rude to not pay attention or even worse, let sushi sit because you're too busy conversing.

- **Oshibori**—This is the warm towel that is served prior to starting the meal. It's a standard practice at all restaurants in Japan (personally wish it was everywhere). It may be an actual towel or perhaps more of a wet wipe if dining at a more casual restaurant. Wipe your hands with it and fold or roll it up nicely when returning onto the holder.

- **Ordering**—Assuming you're sitting at the bar, initially a server might take your order but typically after that, all sushi items will be ordered through the chef. But any other kitchen items or beverages should be ordered through the waitstaff. A good server should be attentive and come by often enough where you wouldn't have to ask the chef. If the restaurant has an omakase course (chef's choice), that's usually the best way to go. Good sushi chefs will take a lot of time and thought into preparing it and take you on a delightful sushi experience from start to finish.

- **Is it rude to ask, "What's fresh"?**—Yes and no. It's rude since those words can imply that the chef is serving something that is not fresh. But the majority of sushi restaurants in the United States are not getting fish flown in fresh daily. Instead, it may be a shipment two to three times per week, which makes the question quite valid. But rather than asking "what's fresh?", a better question might be "What do you recommend?" Important thing is to use your best judgment and always eat sushi at a trusted place.

- **Chopsticks**—Typically it'll be wooden chopsticks that you break apart (high-end restaurants may provide a more formal version). Do not rub them together, you're not trying to start a fire and really when's the last time you seen someone get a splinter in their mouth from chopsticks? If you do see some wood pieces hanging off, just peel that part off or ask for a new pair. Do not pass food from chopstick to chopstick (this includes "cheersing" food with chopsticks as well). In Japanese funerals, special chopsticks are used to pass on the bones of a deceased so for obvious reasons, this is seen as bad luck. Also, never stick chopsticks standing up in a bowl of rice; this represents incense sticks at a funeral and is also considered bad manners.

- **Hands or chopsticks?**—Sushi can be eaten using your hands (sometimes preferred), but sashimi should always be eaten with chopsticks. Nice restaurants will typically bring a small wet towel for you to wipe your fingers.

- **Wasabi**—Traditionally, wasabi is already placed inside each nigiri piece, so there's no need to add more. But if you want some extra kick, take a small amount with your chopsticks and place it on top of your sushi, rather than making a soy sauce slurry. With sashimi, place a bit of wasabi on top of the slice before dipping it in soy sauce.

- **Gari**—Pickled ginger is used as a palate cleanser in between different types of sushi. Eating it with sushi will mask the subtle flavors.
- **How to dip sushi in soy sauce?**—with nigirizushi, dip the fish side lightly into the soy and not the rice. The rice absorbs too much soy sauce, which overpowers the flavor of the piece. Some chefs will brush on a special soy sauce (nikiri shoyu) right before serving each piece (usually at high-end sushi bars), so there's no need to dip it into soy sauce. Gunkanmaki and rolls are a bit different. You can lightly dip the nori side or the corner (for uramaki) into soy sauce, but never dunk or let it sit in it.
- **One bite?**—Yes, sushi is supposed to be enjoyed in one single bite and should be made that way. Good chefs will even make the sharidama (rice ball) slightly smaller for more petite patrons. However, there are many restaurants outside Japan that make their pieces way too large. So, if it's just humanly not possible, then that's not your fault.
- **Finish what you order**—It is rude to not finish your sushi, but I get it, our eyes tend to be bigger than our stomach sometimes and why not just take it home, right? Well, this is dependent on the type of restaurant. If you're sitting at a table and ordering items off of a piece of paper, then it might not matter as much. But let's say

you're sitting in front of the chef, maybe even ordered the omakase (chef's choice), and he/she is serving you piece by piece. Then it will be extremely rude to not finish everything that you're served. That said, a good chef will ask you about any dietary restrictions and/or preference. So, if you don't like wasabi or can't eat any shellfish, you must let them know beforehand. Now that doesn't mean, eat till you puke or take a chance on something you're allergic to. Just know your limit; you can always order more as you go along.

- **Drinking with the chef**—Yes, it's a nice gesture to offer a drink to the chef, more so if you're sitting right in front of them. Obviously it's not required or expected, but it's a great way to get to know each other, especially if you know you're going to frequent the place.
- **Kanpai!**—Standard Japanese toast which loosely translates to "cheers" or "bottoms up." This does not imply you have to one-shot your drink. But you do you on that one . . .
- **Gochisousama deshita**—Is something you typically say at the end of a meal, thanking the chef (or if someone took care of the bill). It loosely translates to "thank you for the meal" and is a nice gesture when you're finished eating or leaving the restaurant. You can also shorten it to just "gochisousama" which is a little more casual. If you can't remember it though, there's nothing wrong with saying "domo arigato"—it's the gesture that counts.

At the end of the day, there are no absolute rules to follow. Do what makes you happy, as everyone has different taste buds and prefers different things. My intention is that the pointers or suggestions I've shared will help you experience a better meal the next time you go to your favorite sushi bar or be less intimidated to go to that Michelin-star sushi spot you've been wanting to go to.

Sushi Glossary

Aburaage—Japanese deep-fried tofu pouch

Amaebi—sweet shrimp

Amaebi no atama—the head of sweet shrimp (often served deep-fried)

Anago—sea eel

Atsuyaki tamago—"thick-cooked" Japanese egg omelet

Awase miso—soyabean paste that combines red and white miso

Barazushi—what chirashi (scattered sushi) is called in the Kansai region of Japan

Buri—a very commonly used fish in Japan that goes by different names depending on its stage in life. Hamachi is a young buri

Chirashi / chirashizushi—scattered-sushi

Chirashi-don—typically a bowl of sushi rice layered with an assortment of colorful cuts of sashimi and vegetables

Daikon—Japanese for "big root," a mild-flavored winter radish

Dashi—family of stocks in Japanese cuisine and is the base for soups, broths, and simmering

Dashimaki tamago—a rolled omelet (like tamagoyaki) with dashi in it

Deba—thick and sturdy knife used to break down whole fish

Domo arigato—"thank you very much"

Donburi—don for short, means bowl

Ebi—shrimp

Edomaezushi—Edo-style sushi

Edo period—period between 1603 and 1867 in the history of Japan, modern sushi was invented during this time

Furikake—rice seasoning

Futomaki—"big roll," a traditional thick and fat sushi roll

Gari—pickled ginger

Gochisousama deshita—loosely translates to "thank you for the meal" and is said as a nice gesture when you're finished eating or leaving the restaurant. You can also shorten it to just "gochisosama," which is a little more casual.

Goma—sesame or sesame seeds

Gunkanmaki—sushi with a strip of seaweed wrapped around, shaped like a battleship

Gyuto—Japanese version of the all-around chef's knife

Hamachi—Japanese amberjack or yellowtail

Hana-age—translates to "flower-fry" and is a traditional cooking method that's used to give tempura more volume and a crispier outer layer

Harasu—belly side of salmon

Hikarimono—shiny-skinned fish

Hinamatsui—girls' day or doll festival

Hinoki—Japanese cypress

Hirame—flounder

Hirazukuri—style/technique of cutting for sashimi that gives you thick, rectangular pieces

Hon-wasabi—real Japanese native wasabi

Hosomaki—translates to thin roll, "hoso" means thin and "maki" means roll

Ikejime—fishing practice where the brain of the fish is immediately pierced after being caught in order to preserve the freshness of the fish

Ikura—salmon roe

Inari—seasoned deep-friend tofu pockets

Irasshaimase—"welcome" or "please come in"

Itadakimasu—"Let's eat," "bon appetit," or "thank you for the food" said before the start of the meal

Itamae—sushi chef

Kaisen-don—seafood bowl

Kaiware daikon—baby radish sprouts

Kani—crab

Kanikama—imitation crab

Kanpai—"cheers" or "bottoms up"

Kanpyo—Japanese gourd

Kansai—southern-central region of Japan's main island Honshu, the Osaka prefecture is located here

Kanto—eastern region of Japan's main island Honshu, the Tokyo prefecture is located here

Kappa—an amphibious, mythological green creature in Japanese folklore, that absolutely loves to eat cucumbers

Kappamaki—cucumber roll

Katsuobushi—dried bonito flakes

Katsuramuki—a peeling technique that creates long, continuous, paper-thin sheets, daikon is commonly used to create a garnish for sashimi dishes

Kinshi tamago—thin shredded strips of an egg crepe

Kizami nori—shredded dried seaweed, used to garnish

Kizami wasabi—chopped and marinated real wasabi stem

Kohada—gizzard shard

Konbu—kelp

Koba—cutting technique that leaves an "edge" by tilting the blade upright at the very end of the cut, typically used for nigirizushi

Kote gaeshi—side flip technique in nigiri

Kurumaebi—Japanese tiger prawn

Kyuri—cucumber

Maguro—tuna

Maki—roll

Makimono—rolled sushi

Makisu—bamboo rolling mat

Makizushi—type of sushi that is rolled

Masago—smelt roe

Me de taberu—translates to "eat with eyes"

Mirin—Japanese sweet rice wine

Miso-shiru / omiso-shiru—miso soup

Moribashi—plating/garnishing chopsticks

Moritsuke—presentation of a dish

Nama—translates to "raw" or "fresh," here it refers to the freshness of Japanese draft beer

Namanarezushi—fish that was consumed before maturation, while still partially raw accompanied with rice

Narezushi—matured sushi

Negi—green onions

Negihama—roll combining green onions and yellowtail

Negitoro—roll combining green onions and toro (fatty tuna)

Neta—topping of the sushi

Nigiri sushi / nigirizushi—combination of sushi rice with a slice of raw fish (typically) on top

Nihon-shu—Japanese sake (rice wine)

Nikiri shoyu—reduced and sweetened soy sauce

Nori—dried seaweed

Omakase—course meal created by the sushi chef

Oshibori—warm towel that is served prior to starting the meal

Oshizushi—sushi that is pressed in a box

Otoro—fatty (belly) bluefin tuna

Otoshibuta—drop lid used to simmer

Ponzu—citrus-based sauce with a tart-tangy flavor, comparable to a vinaigrette

Saba—mackerel

Sake—refers to the general term "alcohol" in Japanese, in the United States it's generally used to refer to Japanese rice wine

Sake / shake—salmon

Saku—fillet that's cut into a block

Sashimi—means "pierced-meat" or "pierced body," referring to the raw fish or meat

Shamoji—rice paddle

Sharidama—rice ball

Shiitake—type of edible mushroom native to Japan

Shinkomaki—Japanese pickled radish roll

Shiso—Japanese perilla leaf

Shoyu—soy sauce

Soba—buckwheat noodles

Sogizukuri—"shave cut" technique for sashimi and nigirizushi

Sujihiki—double-beveled, Western-style version of the yanagiba

Sushi—translates to "sour rice," the vinegared rice that is mixed with other ingredients

Sushi oke (hangiri)—wooden sushi mixing bowl or tub

Tai—sea bream

Takuwan—Japanese pickled radish

Tamago—egg

Tamagoyaki—general Japanese term for a rolled omelet and is a staple in Japanese cuisine

Tatemaki—vertical roll

Tekka—translates to "iron fire," sparks generated during forging. Also short for tekkamaki

Tekka-ba—popular gambling halls in the late Edo period

Tekkamaki—tuna roll

Temari—Japanese embroidered balls called "temari," which translates to "hand-ball." It was originally made for children's games like hacky sack. Now it's used more for decorative ornaments.

Temaki / temakizushi—hand roll

Temari sushi / temarizushi—variety of nigirizushi that is rolled into a ball

Tempura—lightly battered seafood or vegetables that's deep-fried until it has a golden, crispy shell

Tempurako—tempura flour

Tendon—tempura donburi or tempura bowl

Tezu / temizu—mixture of water and rice vinegar

Tobiko—flying fish roe

Tsuma—finely sliced daikon that is used to garnish raw fish

Udon—a thick noodle made from wheat flour, used in Japanese cuisine

Umami—savory or meaty tastes of food, one of the five basic tastes

Unagi—freshwater eel

Unagi no tare—Japanese BBQ sauce used for freshwater eel

Uni—sea urchin

Uramaki—inside-out rolls

Usuba bocho—Japanese thin vegetable knife

Usuyaki tamago—paper-thin omelette

Usuzukuri—thinner cut of sogizukuri

Uzura—quail egg

Wakame—type of seaweed

Wasabi—can refer to "hon" wasabi (real wasabi made from the rhizome of the Wasabia Japonica plant) or imitation wasabi, which is typically made from horseradish

Yanagiba—long and narrow blade knife that is most commonly used for sushi

Yuzu—fragrant and sour citrus that originates from Eastern Asia

Index

Conversion Charts

METRIC AND IMPERIAL CONVERSIONS

(These conversions are rounded for convenience)

Ingredient	Cups/Tablespoons/ Teaspoons	Ounces	Grams/Milliliters
Butter	1 cup/ 16 tablespoons/ 2 sticks	8 ounces	230 grams
Cheese, shredded	1 cup	4 ounces	110 grams
Cornstarch	1 tablespoon	0.3 ounce	8 grams
Cream cheese	1 tablespoon	0.5 ounce	14.5 grams
Flour, all-purpose	1 cup/1 tablespoon	4.5 ounces/0.3 ounce	125 grams/8 grams
Flour, whole wheat	1 cup	4 ounces	120 grams
Fruit, dried	1 cup	4 ounces	120 grams
Fruits or veggies, chopped	1 cup	5 to 7 ounces	145 to 200 grams
Fruits or veggies, pureed	1 cup	8.5 ounces	245 grams
Honey, maple syrup, or corn syrup	1 tablespoon	0.75 ounce	20 grams
Liquids: cream, milk, water, or juice	1 cup	8 fluid ounces	240 milliliters
Oats	1 cup	5.5 ounces	150 grams
Salt	1 teaspoon	0.2 ounce	6 grams
Spices: cinnamon, cloves, ginger, or nutmeg (ground)	1 teaspoon	0.2 ounce	5 milliliters
Sugar, brown, firmly packed	1 cup	7 ounces	200 grams
Sugar, white	1 cup/1 tablespoon	7 ounces/0.5 ounce	200 grams/12.5 grams
Vanilla extract	1 teaspoon	0.2 ounce	4 grams

OVEN TEMPERATURES

Fahrenheit	Celsius	Gas Mark
225°	110°	¼
250°	120°	½
275°	140°	1
300°	150°	2
325°	160°	3
350°	180°	4
375°	190°	5
400°	200°	6
425°	220°	7
450°	230°	8